FIND THE WAY
BACK TO *You*
WITH
LOLA LOLA

How to Thrive in Life
after Surviving
Sexual Abuse

YANETTE NOVOA, LCSW

BALBOA.PRESS
A DIVISION OF HAY HOUSE

Balboa Press books may be ordered through booksellers or by contacting:

Balboa Press
A Division of Hay House
1663 Liberty Drive
Bloomington, IN 47403
www.balboapress.com
844-682-1282

Because of the dynamic nature of the Internet, any web addresses or links contained in this book may have changed since publication and may no longer be valid. The views expressed in this work are solely those of the author and do not necessarily reflect the views of the publisher, and the publisher hereby disclaims any responsibility for them.

The author of this book does not dispense medical advice or prescribe the use of any technique as a form of treatment for physical, emotional, or medical problems without the advice of a physician, either directly or indirectly. The intent of the author is only to offer information of a general nature to help you in your quest for emotional and spiritual well-being. In the event you use any of the information in this book for yourself, which is your constitutional right, the author and the publisher assume no responsibility for your actions.

Any people depicted in stock imagery provided by Getty Images are models, and such images are being used for illustrative purposes only. Certain stock imagery © Getty Images.

Edited by: Janette Colomer-Maurii

Print information available on the last page.

ISBN: 979-8-7652-4628-3 (sc)
ISBN: 979-8-7652-4630-6 (hc)
ISBN: 979-8-7652-4629-0 (e)

Library of Congress Control Number: 2023919489

Balboa Press rev. date: 12/13/2023

This self-help guide is dedicated to the children
and the many still in silence.

It takes courage to push yourself to places that you have never been before ... to test your limits ... to break through barriers. And the day came when the risk it took to remain tight inside the bud was more painful than the risk it took to blossom.

—*Anais Nin*

CONTENTS

ACKNOWLEDGMENTS

Special thanks to my youngest sister, the wind beneath my wings, Jhousy, friend in heaven, Teresa, and best friend and sister on this earth (Natalie) for believing in me at each phase of my life and without judgement. To my girls, grandson, nieces, nephews, and all children, I dedicate this song: "I Hope You Dance" by Lee Ann Womack. Thanks to my husband for the continual encouragement. And most importantly, to my mother, Rose, who has made sure that I am a tough cookie to break, both with her presence and lack thereof. Thank you!

INTRODUCTION

There are 42 million survivors of childhood sexual abuse in the United States, with approximately 20 percent of sexual abuse victims being younger than eight years of age. What is most disastrous is that 90 percent of sexual abuse victims know the perpetrator in some way.

Sexual abuse is a raging problem in America today, and it has been for a long time. The target audience for this book is the younger and older adults, male and female, who have had to experience such an ordeal; are in search of acceptance and healing; and know that thriving after such an experience is possible. In its own unique way, this book also attempts to make caregivers to the vulnerable child, adult, and elderly person aware of the problem, which in and of itself can serve as a prevention tool.

Please note that Lola Lola is a pseudonym, a name that came out of my desperation to find myself, which will be explained later in pages 15–17 of this introduction.

I lived moments of rape from the age of four to twelve, ending up with an illegal abortion at the age of twelve in the presence of the perpetrator—a person I loved and thought of as a father figure, who forever changed my life. At the time of the abortion, I saw the face of human cruelty when I was taken to that sterile and cold room where you are supposed to be put to rest after such ordeal. There I had my first experience with what it feels like to be discriminated against by the public who fail to see beyond certain individual circumstances and are quick to judge the surface without looking deeper.

That day, a piece of me just collapsed into nothingness. The doctor's eye of judgment, along with the surgical swab being pulled out of me, left me with a sense of shame, guilt, disgust, and unworthiness. This event transformed me into a living defense mechanism, a survival-mode girl, ready to react with the hurting heart that was built by the unconsciously devastating effects that this experience had left me with.

In my own definition, the moment you make a sexual advance toward a child or any vulnerable individual, you have committed rape. You are automatically raping that individual or child of their basic human rights. The moment an individual touches a child in an inappropriate sexual manner, it is rape: rape of the child's rights as a human being, specifically the right to respect and dignity.

Children have rights! They have the right to say *no*, the right to have a normal childhood without any type of abuse, the right to explore their own sexual orientation or preference issues when they are ready and with whom they want. Anybody who touches a child inappropriately is raping that child out of a normal childhood. That child is being forced to view the world differently, through painful, not-trusting, scared, confused, and angry eyes. At that moment, life for a child or any person becomes dull and scary. It is scary to trust and believe that individuals are like this person who raped you.

Inconceivably, after this atrocious experience, it is far too common that victimized persons do not believe or understand that they are the victim. They are left feeling guilty because in some way, they think that they provoked the perpetrator. It is then that silence may become a way of life.

I was oblivious to the fact that I was indeed a victim and that I could speak out without shame and guilt. Finally, via many voices, but in particular Dr. Maya Angelou's, I learned that it was perfectly fine to relate my story in the hope that I might become, as she would put it, "a rainbow in someone's cloud."

I was not a sexy girl or a seductive child attracted to men, as I have heard even women say. I was a child victimized by an adult who knew exactly what he was doing. I had no voice, no one to give true support, and no one to understand me. For a long time, I had been the "make everyone happy" person, and yes, I was angry! I was angry for a long time and felt and still feel disgusted every time I think about the fact that as we speak, there are children being sexually abused, and most likely by someone they know, trust, and yes, *love*.

Loving the person who is hurting you usually goes hand in hand, as in most cases this person is a family member—someone who is supposed to love, protect, and support you and not take advantage of your love. Thus, the problem of sexual abuse will never be completely solved until there is no child or person with the potential for being sexually abused.

Imagine living with such internal confusion between anger, guilt, deception, and much more. Not to count your daily need to survive within a community you have a somewhat distorted perception of that may not be the truth about humans at all. Imagine getting by at work and school, raising a child, being part of a team, and interacting with family members—all with false perceptions of what relationships really are or should be.

Picture a relationship with your significant other in which you are in no place to give the love that is supposed to overflow from you for that relationship to work but instead are so needy you may consume your partner, to the point of drying that person out. What kind of relationship would that be? Can a person with such inner turmoil really live a happy and fulfilled life?

I was not so conscious of my own turmoil and feelings of shame or guilt playing a leading role in each and every situation I encountered—specifically my interactions with people, especially those in a role of authority. I feared all people in general, and yet I was reflecting anger. Consciously, the fear of authority figures and the inevitable need to help and thrive as an individual left me with no other way out but to share my story and strategies used with the hope to be a rainbow in someone's cloud.

Thus, for the past ten to fifteen years of my life, if I may say, self-analysis has been a thorough and painful process, and rest assured that it continues. I started looking into where my life was at and where it was headed exactly. I took the time to observe the person who was to become Lola Lola, to stop and notice my own patterns of behaviors and thoughts that perhaps were contributing to having the wrong situations or people in my life.

I started noticing that perhaps there could be some things in my perception of the people and the world itself that needed changing. I came to a halt when I suddenly realized that this had conditioned me to have a high abuse tolerance, allowing constant disrespect and abuse from family and friends I so eagerly wanted to be accepted by.

The need to question these perceptions was unavoidable. I started considering that maybe, all this time, I had been wrong in my own way of seeing certain situations and my judgment towards others. I came to the realization that my need to please others was becoming detrimental to my physical and mental health. Finally, I accepted the fact that I was not that OK. This understanding was mind-blowing, automatically adding to my internal turmoil, to my shame, as I was always right and there was no conceivable way I could have been wrong about anything all this time.

Inspired by the possibility that I was "faulty," I bombarded myself with extensive research and degrees, and worked with individual victims of sexual abuse until slowly I began to internalize, understand, and accept many of the terms and/or phrases that will be presented to you in this guide. I am certain this guide will set the stage for you to find your own true voice all over again, as I did.

However, you should know that none of it prepared me as much as the years I spent in silence, in shame, and guilt. As awful as this may sound, at the end of your journey, you will discover how these feelings are the driving force behind your many accomplishments. They will give you the needed courage to make a change in your own life. Thus, the making of Lola Lola has been the hardest thing I have ever done but the most rewarding indeed.

When family, colleagues, or friends would, for some reason, mention this topic, I would hide in my shell, not knowing why, yet intuitively knowing that one day I would need to address this part of my life somehow. To this day, I hold the belief that not until we truly confront ourselves, acknowledging, and accepting our own being, can we really become who we are meant to become. This is what I intend to inspire you to do. I want this guide to be your turning point—the point at which you recognize the need for change, acknowledge your current resources, and build from that. The end result will be a new, booming you.

Reading books such as *I'm OK, You're OK* by Dr. Thomas A. Harris also assisted in my constant questioning of myself. Dr. Harris was born in Texas in 1910. He was a practicing psychiatrist and sold millions of copies of this book, which was eventually translated into twenty different languages. The book was based on transactional analysis, developed by Dr. Eric Berne in his bestseller *Games People Play* in 1964.[1]

In general, Dr. Harris wrote that most people live their lives in a state of negativism. Dr. Harris referred to living out in the negative, stemming from the mindset of *I'm not OK, you're OK*. The latter may cause people to behave as victims giving way to dysfunctional emotional reactions, mainly situating ourselves within the victim role. With his book, Dr. Harris encouraged us to adapt to an *I'm OK, You're OK*, mindset. For Dr. Harris, being OK with yourself and with others is the way to happiness, personal fulfillment, and adequate relationships. Thus, I adamantly continued to ask myself if I was OK.

This idea of being OK also led me to the understanding that at no moment should a lost job, an experience of any type of abuse, a lost house, and/or a lost car or relationship be a definition of who you are as a person. Nothing that ever happens to us is a definition of who we are. Different experiences take place so we can shift our focus back on our conscious journey to better ourselves and to remain as humble as we can. The faster and the better we learn from it, the more resilient and happy a person we become.

However, without a doubt, it is a rocky and emotionally challenging task. This is the same thing that many of the best poets, prophets, and gurus want to convey to us within their own unique way of expressing themselves. Simply put, having been sexually abused will never be a definition of who you are as a person. You are a person who will have

---

[1] . Nicholas Berne Calceterra, "Thomas A. Harris M.D., Author *I'm OK-You're OK*," revised 2023, http://www.drthomasharris.com.

negative and positive experiences, and as for anyone else, it is a part of a learning process in this so-called life.

As a side note, if you are concerned about the opinion of those around you, just know that what others think can be a *disablement* to your life if you are not aware that their opinions are not your problem. What others think should not be of concern, as in most cases what we perceive from others or what others perceive from us is a mere reflection of who we or they are as persons.

Let what others think or do be their problem, not yours. Let others deal with their own evils, and you deal with yours. Understanding this was imperative in my journey to being OK.

Being sexually abused as a child and for so long was an experience for me that, if given the choice, I would not have picked, as its effects can indeed be devastating. You spend most of your life asking yourself, "What would my childhood, adolescence, and adult life have been like if this would not have happened to me?" However, to some degree, I am thankful for it, as it has made me the person I find writing this guide—a person who can look someone in the eyes and feel their hurt; a person who can feel life; a person who is human, is present, and can enjoy the small moments with far greater joy and acceptance than ever before. It's an experience from which you can learn a lot about how to become a better helping person.

Before I gained an ability to trust, confiding in someone was well beyond my capacity. My sense of self–respect had been tampered with, and my self-esteem was diminished. I had two individuals to whom I owed a lot, or so I thought: my sister and brother. Everything I did had always been with them in the back of my mind. I naively thought that I needed to get an education for them to be OK; I needed to make it for *them*. Then, when my daughters were born, I needed to continue my education for them as well. In my mind, they needed to be OK, so I bettered myself for them via education.

That was my definition of bettering myself—getting an education. However, as important as this may be for some, it is not the essence of being OK. I still had not really understood what Dr. Harris had said *I'm OK, You're OK*. I needed to be OK, and for me, that meant I needed to be an emotionally stable individual capable of maintaining healthy relationships and finding my own happiness and personal satisfaction.

Was I an OK mother, sister, employee? Was I aware of who I represented as a human being? And the ultimate question: was I happy? Getting an education may have opened up more opportunities within the workforce, and it may have allowed for a more financially stable life, but it didn't necessarily mean that I was OK and they were OK.

I never realized when I set out on my quest to get an education that what I really needed to be OK was to confront and come to terms with myself, the emotional being. Reaching emotional stability is the most crucial factor in determining whether you are OK now and will continue to be in the future.

When we choose a husband, a career, a hobby, a house, a life journey, or a job, we should first make sure that we are OK. Your family and friends will need the best version of you—a version that sees the world as "I'm OK, You're OK." Only then will your ability to interact with others become a smooth and fulfilling process. And then *they* will be OK, as their emotional stability is just a reflection of yours.

In Maslow's self-actualizing theory (hierarchy of needs), he suggests and describes in ranked order the basics that we need to have accomplished before becoming self-actualized individuals: physiological, safety, love/belonging, esteem, and self-actualization. *Physiological* is number one in the ranking and is described as breathing, food, sex, sleep, etc. For example, Maslow suggests that for you to go to the safety rank, you first need to have your physiological needs met.[2]

I found Maslow to be on point with this hierarchy of needs. However, during these years of observation and painful growth, I have observed that safety, love/belonging, and esteem should be happening concurrently with the physiological rank. In other words, they should be happening at the same time, and not in succession, if individuals are to even consider becoming that self-actualized person they so desire to be.

I have observed that safety, social, and self-esteem needs all

---

[2] . Joaquin Selva, "What Is Self-Actualization? Meaning, Theory + Examples," *Positive Psychology*, May 5, 2017, https://positivepsychology.com/self-actualization/.

contribute to a balanced emotional well-being. Over the years, I have learned that a healthy emotional balance or emotional intelligence, as some may say, should develop simultaneously with having your physiological needs met, if not before. For individuals to succeed, they cannot be without either one. If one is lacking, we will eventually die. Without food, we will die, and yet with food but without emotional balance (safety, social, and self-esteem needs), we can live an unfulfilled life that will ultimately kill us.

To have emotional balance, we need to feel safe, have adequate self-esteem, have a clear self-concept, have been adequately nurtured, feel a sense of belonging, feel a part of a community, have a strong support system, have a roof over our heads, and have food to eat, to mention a few. Which of the two is worse to feel a lack of, physiological or emotional needs? You pick. For me, it is obvious that a lack of the latter is much worse.

Have you seen men and women who, despite their wealth, live unfulfilled lives? Can you explain how, if their physiological needs are met and they appear to be self-actualized individuals, they still live miserable lives? Can you explain the death of celebrities like Robin Williams, Kate Spade, and Anthony Bourdain? Can you explain the life of Michael Jackson, who was the icon of pop music, yet his behaviors revealed his unrestful attempt to find emotional stability during all his adult life? Instead, he found early death. Can you explain his ambiguity toward his sexual preference and allegations of child sexual abuse that, without question, made way for his self-destructive habits and perhaps the destruction of those around him who loved him deeply?

During my ongoing attempt to find the way back to the emotional, thriving me—and also inspired by the American inspirational speaker Iyanla Vanzant—the ideal me, Lola Lola, initiated the process of becoming a thriving individual. At this time, I also started asking, "What kind of person are you? Do you already have some preexisting qualities that define you, such as polite, respectful, ethical—and even if you have them, are you really displaying them? What person do you want others to see? What do you want to see?" I started gathering information about who I wanted to be viewed as, which is part of what this guide intends to have you accomplish.

I started observing the different interactions of my colleagues, family members, and friends I truly admired. I wondered, *Why do I admire them?* I observed patiently to see how their reactions were and how they treated themselves and others.

For example, I noted how one of my colleagues was always prudent and would treat other colleagues with respect. She would treat her clients as human beings and, in my opinion, with the same dignity and respect she would use if the president of the United States would suddenly walk in the room. When no one was looking (but I was), she displayed the same values, treating herself and others with the utmost dignity.

Through many observations thereafter, I decided that Lola Lola would have manners, be kind, have integrity (be the same individual in private as in public), keep her word, practice patience, think twice about how to speak to others, and manage her own anger. Obviously, Lola Lola is still in the making, yet she is now a long stretch from the person she used to be. Lola Lola continues to work hard to become her ideal individual, along with her daily task to look within and make sure her physiological needs are parallel with her emotional state. Only when those needs are completely cared for can we become the thriving individuals that we want to become.

I have experienced the pain that the depths of depression bring, and I know how it feels to be in a world full of shame, guilt, and ongoing self-doubt. I have also had the experience—and if I may, *adventure*— of learning how others who experience sexual abuse, either in their childhoods or in their later years, have dealt with trials in remarkably different ways, with the same goal to survive. Only a small percentage see their quest as not to survive but to thrive in life.

During my years of gathering information, I could not help but notice that there is ample space between *surviving* and *thriving*. The individuals who choose to take their walk toward thriving have been shown to live richer and more fulfilled lives than those who choose to just survive. Therefore, this guide was also completed with the idea of helping you clarify for yourself just what phase you may be in at present, and to consciously decide which of the two roads to take: surviving or thriving.

This guide will provide you with the necessary techniques to solve your problems and help you get to the place within that you would like to be, and where life would be seen as it is: *beautiful!* With the ups and downs, the ugly and the pretty, the complex and the simple, life is beautiful.

In this guide, I go to the basics and present to you the identifying phases to find a way that can work to assist you in going back to your essence. That may be a difficult task to accomplish; thus, the phases presented offer a path to self-analysis, leading the way to finding emotional balance, which in turn serves as the basis for finding the thriving you. Finding the *thriving* you can also, later on in life's journey, relate to reaching transcendence, which Maslow described in his later years before he died as finding purpose aside from oneself.[3] You can use these phases as a measuring scale to see where you stand in your relationship with yourself and others, identify your problem-solving patterns, learn how you have dealt with your abuse, and recognize incongruences with your behavior and ability to keep emotional balance.

My find-the-way phases describe general definitions that you may be familiar with, such as the meaning of *victim, survivor* (survive), *accomplisher* (accomplish), *striver* (strive), and *thriving* (thrive). These terms may be familiar, but do you understand their meaning? It is almost like the concept of, you see the flowers, but have you stopped to smell and truly experience those flowers and their wonder? Have you really acknowledged or internalized these concepts?

Once these terms are truly internalized, you find yourself with questions like the following: *How much information do I have about children and the long-term effects of sexual abuse? Do I know that the longer I go without coming to terms with my abuse, and the longer I keep or stay in silence without focusing on helping myself, the longer I will keep re-victimizing myself in many different and subtle ways?*

---

[3] . Kyle Kowalski, "What Is Transcendence? The True Top of Maslow's Hierarchy of Needs," *Sloww*, June 15, 2023, https://www.sloww.co/transcendence-maslow/.

I say *subtle* because you may be subconsciously reacting to certain situations, and you may find yourself asking, *Why does this keep happening to me? Am I in some way attracting these situations into my life?* Then, what will you do about this?

It was once read to me from the Bible that there is a time for everything—a time to cry, a time to laugh, and a time to play. You have had enough time to feel shameful and guilty about something that has never been your fault. You have been in denial for so long, thinking that there is something wrong with you and perhaps subconsciously ashamed of saying your truth.

Well, I am not telling you to come out right now and announce, "Ohhh, by the way, I was sexually abused as a child." That is not what I am saying, but I *am* saying to remember that there is a time for everything, and that like all big stories in the news—such as the incident with former President Bill Clinton in the Oval Office—people will react in the moment, but after a few days, they will be reacting to something else taking place and will forget what you said, will laugh, or will acknowledge it and respect you for it and then move to another story.

In other words, you are so scared to be who you are or voice your experiences because of your own perceptions of yourself, people, and community that you may be losing time to focus on other topics, such as your dreams. Things are simpler than you think. You are a human being who was victimized, and this guide will simplify terms that you already know and guide you into finding your way toward your own personal fulfillments.

This guide will assist you in acknowledging that you are an important piece in this so-called life and the better equipped you are, the faster you will find your place in the puzzle. Consider that the sooner you find your place, the sooner you can make way for others to find theirs as well. Then life will suddenly become easier, smoother, and nicer, even in those harsh moments, because you will have learned to live. Thus, ask yourself, what time is it now and for whom?

It took me ten to eighteen years to finally sit down and write about my personal learning experience with sexual abuse and the journey towards identifying myself as a thriving individual. The quest to find my true self, the becoming of Lola Lola, has been the best gift I have ever given myself. It has and continues to be a challenge in and of itself. However, it took an awful long time, which limits the years that you can enjoy the company of the thriving you.

One of the main goals of this guide, if not the main one, is for you to make a conscious decision to not take so long to become who you aspire to be. As the saying goes, if life gives you lemons, learn to make lemonade and enjoy it. Do not take so long to be happy, shame-free, without guilt, or in love with yourself, life, or people, as while you struggle with the effects of your trauma, life is happening.

This guide will also provide you with stories about famous people who overcame bad experiences and were able to find their thriving selves, to illustrate key points. Further, this guide also contains exercises and questionnaires to assist you in your journey to a better life. Ask if it is fair for you not to be, daily, in complete awe of yourself. Knowing that our experiences are just there for us to learn to be humbler and overall better human beings can set the stage for change.

I now leave you to the pages of this guide that have been completed with all the love and tears you can possibly imagine. By making the decision to help yourself, you will be indirectly helping the many who are still in silence to eventually join the many of us who are in the fight to prevent and, with undying hope, stop child sexual abuse against any individual regardless of their race, gender, culture, and/or socio-economic status. Just by your action of consistently bettering yourself, you will motivate others to do the same.

Are you ready for your journey? It may not seem that way now, but this is going to be the most exciting time of your life. You will live, you will question everything and everyone, and you will learn to say no, to say yes, and mean it. You will learn to love. You will learn to observe in stillness and, when needed, to let go with great ease those things that no longer serve a purpose for you.

You will finally have the courage to say what you think and maybe stop what has been going on for generations in your family. You will finally address the elephant in the room and be OK with the ruffling of feathers even within your own family unit. You will be there without judgment or criticism, offering your unconditional love to yourself. And this is just wonderful!

I urge you to make an active decision to start, willingly and consciously, the process of acceptance of all—to let go and move on to a better you. This is the fun part: letting go and moving on. It opens you to the real world and allows you to start feeling, giving, and loving in a whole new way. You will find yourself saying, "OMG! And I took so long?"

Lola Lola is inviting you to find the best yet, to discover part of you that will eventually live life with a completely blissful sense of accomplishment. In the process of being Lola Lola, I have found that I can be *me* more and more each day without the constant shame. And trust me—it is kind of formidable to finally accept who and what we represent.

This self-journey has been a gift that continues to endure, and one I will not need to throw away or put away somewhere to gather dust. It is a gift I utilize to make my life and that of others better in every feasible way. Do I mess up sometimes? *Yes*, but always a little less than before. No matter how you look at it, if you decide to continue with your journey, it will be the greatest gift you can give yourself and others. To that I can attest!

CHAPTER 1

FIND-THE-WAY PHASES

My find-the-way phases will guide you in becoming the thriving individual you envision yourself to be, the person who has been waiting to be completely free—free of self-doubt, free of self-criticism, free of self-destructive behaviors. You will free the negative self and all condemnation to effortlessly be you, the thriving individual.

These phases offer a way to identify your present stance so that you can make a conscious decision as to how you want to be identified for the remainder of your human experience:

- Phase 1: The Victim
- Phase 2: The Survivor
- Phase 3: The Accomplisher
- Phase 4: The Striver
- Phase 5: The Thriver

PHASE 1: THE VICTIM

Recognize that you were a victim—emphasis on the word *were*. And understand that you have been affected and that your perception of humanity and relationships, in general, may not be that realistic. This is a wake-up call! Acknowledging that you *were* a victim will eventually help you break free from the feeling of guilt.

For those who have experienced sexual abuse, it may take a whole lifetime to understand that they were indeed the victim of such a despicable act. Once this has been identified, it will be time to start getting informed, accepting, and acknowledging that you were abused. That is the time for you to start working on yourself.

Before we move on, we will review the definition of *victim* as a point of reflection on what constitutes being a victim of sexual abuse.

How Do You Know You Were a Victim?

It would be natural to assume that children who are sexually abused would understand they were the victim. However, if they had known, they would not have become victims in the first place. Children or adults victimized by a parent, a boyfriend, a friend, an uncle, etc., may feel a sort of responsibility. They may feel that to a certain degree they contributed to their abuse by something they did or said, or their desire to be accepted and loved. Thus, comes the feeling of guilt often associated with victims of sexual abuse.

Another factor that keeps the child or adult victims of sexual abuse from understanding what being a victim is, is the fact that 90 percent of the time, the perpetrator is a family member—a person you love and want understanding and love from. Imagine the confusion that may stem from this fact alone in the mind of a young person and even a grown adult. An adult person violated by an ex-boyfriend or a person they are currently dating may be confused between feelings of having been violated versus continuous questioning of, *Did I cause this somehow? Were my clothes too revealing? Was I flirting too much? Should I not have gone to the hotel with that person?*

These questions circulating in the brain of people who were indeed victimized may give rise to a sort of feeling of guilt and shame, as to some degree they would think they contributed to the abuse. Thus, the inclination toward not reporting the abuse and deciding to remain quiet, which in the long run will contribute to an increase in the person's level of tolerance to abuse of any kind. It becomes a vicious cycle and another viable reason why children who have been abused once are often the victims of repeated abuse.

It is highly likely within certain families that children have been the victim of sexual abuse by different family members, but because of many concepts and broken boundaries, understanding how they are being victimized may become difficult. Instead, they may have the understanding that this is normal behavior for the individuals who love them. So where is the understanding that this individual was victimized, and when does normalized behavior stop? Thus, the cycle continues.

This points out the importance of education and the need to internalize the meaning of *victim*. According to Merriam-Webster, a *victim* is a person who has been attacked, injured, robbed, or killed by someone else; a person who is cheated or fooled by someone else; and someone who is harmed by an unpleasant event (such as an illness or accident).[4]

Think: A child who has been a victim of sexual abuse has been robbed of something of immense value—the ability to trust, respect in, believe in, and confide in themselves, let alone others. And let's not even talk about their innocence. An individual who has experienced sexual abuse at an early age or at any point in life has been robbed of innocence, the right to make decisions, and the right for self-respect and dignity.

PHASE 2: THE SURVIVOR

If you find yourself identifying with this second phase, you understand that you have survived a terrible, life-impacting experience, and somehow you are still on hold. You are stagnant and unable to function at your optimum level—the *thriving* you. You are vulnerable yet without the tools to manage that vulnerability. In other words, you are left vulnerable to being revictimized, as is the case when you are without the necessary tools to thrive.

---

[4] . "Victim," Merriam-Webster Dictionary, https://www.merriam-webster.com/dictionary/victim.

You are not fully conscious of yourself and are just in survival mode. You are getting through the day, with little to show for it. The fact that you have survived this terrible experience and continue to get by at work, at school, or in society is something that deserves recognition and is without a doubt something to be extremely proud of. Yes, pat yourself on the back as you function and survive daily against all odds.

Nevertheless, once you accept that you have survived, and you are functioning daily, it is imperative that you start to challenge and confront your innermost true feelings and current situation. Ask yourself as many of these questions as you need:

- Am I happy now?
- Am I truly doing things for me, to help myself reach my objectives or goals?
- How are my current relationships?
- What mistakes or misconceptions have caused chaos in my life?
- What do I expect of others and of myself?
- Who am I?
- What do I want?
- How do I want others to view me, or do I care?
- How do I care for others?
- What differences have I made?
- At what point of my life am I?
- Am I truly 100 percent content with how I do things and where am I headed?
- Am I merely surviving, or am I genuinely happy, self-confident, and/or living a fulfilled life?
- What is a fulfilled life for me?
- How has this terrible experience in my developing years caused me to have irrational perceptions of society and/or myself?
- Am I truly whole, or are there parts of my actions that I or those around me would benefit from me working on?
- Am I that thriving individual, the one content with where and how life is playing out?

- Am I a survivor who may still be vulnerable or at risk of being revictimized?
- Am I a survivor, one who merely makes it through the day because of all the baggage that keeps me from becoming a thriving individual?
- Am I a survivor who depends on others to coexist, to function?
- Am I a survivor who is dependent upon any kind of chemical to make it through the day?

If when answering these questions, you notice a minimal feeling of dissatisfaction and/or disappointment within you and know in your gut that you can do more to change your circumstances, then you know you are merely surviving, and you may well benefit from asking yourself if it would be beneficial for you to seek deeper in search of those answers.

First, let's revisit what it means to be a survivor. The American Heritage Dictionary defines *survivor* generally as someone or something that continues to exist, to function, after misfortune or trauma.[5] Despite the traumatic event, you continue to exist, function, and live on.

Answering these questions will put you in a tough situation with yourself. I have been there, but it is OK. To confront your own inner demons, as some say, will be one of the most heroic acts you will find yourself doing in your lifetime, and many will thank you for it someday.

Also—trust me on this—just surviving has been a heroic act, but now you will move beyond this. At the end of the day, every experience or situation that comes into your life does so with a purpose, with a teaching, or with a message. But you must look closely to catch on, and perhaps you will not be able to if you are too busy merely surviving.

Look beyond the physical—your present education, your home, your spouse, and your material gathering—and investigate whether you would feel whole without any of those things. If in doing this search, you see yourself identifying with phase two, then you are what I call a survivor. Yes, as previously indicated, you deserve congratulations, as

---

5 . "Survivor," The American Heritage Dictionary, https://www.ahdictionary.com/word/search.html?q=survivor.

you are surviving and/or functioning daily in a society that can be a bit scary. But there is definitely more.

Keep asking those questions:

- Am I really living?
- Am I accomplishing, striving, or thriving?
- Am I truly doing what I want?
- Am I truly an accomplisher of what I want?
- Am I truly striving to reach my goals?
- Am I really a thriving individual?
- How much longer until I reunite with myself?
- Would I feel better or be happier if I came to terms with who I truly am?

Oh boy, there is work to do! Knowing who you are delivers you from so much accumulated or yet-to-accumulate garbage, it is not even funny. We walk around with too much garbage that was not meant for us in the first place. So ask yourself—are you ready to let it go? And remember, there is more to learn, more to experience, more to create, more to live, more to feel, more to love, more to give, and more to life.

There is more!

What is your choice? Post your answer on the mirror of your bathroom or anywhere you can see it daily.

PHASE 3: THE ACCOMPLISHER

See yourself more as an accomplisher: a person capable of accomplishing things and taking the initiative to start.

Among Merriam-Webster's definitions of *accomplish* is, "1. to bring about ... 3. To succeed in reaching (a stage in a progression)."[6] Identifying yourself as an accomplisher is like saying, "Well, I went

---

[6] . "Accomplish," Merriam-Webster Dictionary, https://www.merriam-webster.com/dictionary/accomplish.

through this experience, and I survived." But now you need to identify your (realistic) dreams; you need to start setting small but reachable goals; and you need to start seeing yourself more as an accomplisher (a person capable of accomplishing things).

Say to yourself, *I am a person capable of accomplishing that which I have set forth. I am not just a victim or survivor of sexual abuse.* Now you are an individual with goals who will not merely survive but follow your dreams. Now you have moved past being a victim and a survivor to being an accomplisher.

Accomplishers understand that any abuse endured does not identify who they are. During your answering of the many questions that you will have for yourself, you will learn that no experience, good or bad, in its essence, will ever be able to identify who you are. Once you are aware of this phenomenon, no traumatic experience will ever play a major role in your life for too long a time, and right away you will look for the learning opportunity in each. If we are aware, we can learn from any experience, however traumatic, and move past it with newly acquired and valuable awareness.

PHASE 4: THE STRIVER

You identify yourself as a striving individual: an individual capable of exerting much effort daily toward reaching your goals and dreams. The Cambridge Academic Content Dictionary defines *striving* as "to try hard to do something or making something happen, esp. for a long time or against difficulties."[7]

In all these steps and stages, there will be an experiencing of doubt along with many other emotions. However, the striver has developed effective coping strategies to maintain the needed emotional balance. The striver recognizes that emotions are not facts or opinions but are there to be welcomed with the full understanding that it is OK to feel

---

[7] . "Striving," Cambridge Academic Content Dictionary, Cambridge University Press.

them to quickly observe the reason for their place in our heart. Like that, we can acknowledge our urgent need to be on our toes and go through these emotions as smoothly and coolly as possible.

For this, you need to surround yourself with things, people, videos, movies, etc. that inspire movement, that ignite passion and perseverance. Dance and music can take you far and can bring you back to your true nature. For me, such an inspiring dance video would be Jennifer Lopez's medley opening performance at the American Music Awards of 2015, showing the transitioning of dance moves upon the changing of music. If we are going to eventually thrive, it is by going with the waves and transitioning through the divergent phases of life that will bring us to success. Remember that you call the shots, not anyone else.

This does not mean to fight but to strive each day. There is no need to feel as if you are fighting. Fighting signals weakness and self-doubt, with the constant need to prove to others who and what you are. It can feel as if you are going against the current when instead, you can work hard every day yet enjoy the present moment while maintaining your calm and cool. By remaining calm and going with the current, you can see your goals and objectives clearly. You will also learn from your experiences at a quicker rate.

If you find yourself identifying as a striver, think of yourself as a cat. Cats self-clean and in the process remove dead fur and the smell of food from their whiskers and fur, reducing potential encounters with possible predators. When cats self-clean, they also reduce the potential for fleas/parasites, help their circulation, regulate body temperature, and even speed healing if injured. Like the cat, we humans can engage in self-reflection, which can help us in becoming more aware when we engage in negative or positive self-talk, feelings, actions, and emotions.

Self-reflection can also assist in noticing our feelings when around certain individuals, and whether or not these individuals are having a positive impact on our lives. The latter is of utmost importance, as the individuals we have around us can either keep us from reaching our true potential or promote our willingness to continue working toward becoming our best self.

As with the cat, self-reflection during the healing process can also assist us in maintaining good health. Thus, self-cleaning and/or self-reflection can keep us on the right track in our journey and may help in setting reachable goals.

Falling and/or losing track of your goals may and will occasionally be inevitable. However, self-cleaning and self-reflection, as with the cat, will help in allowing you to never stop moving toward your goal. At this point, you are striving, not fighting. You are calmly and coolly reaching your objectives and going with the current.

PHASE 5: THE THRIVER

Identifying yourself as a *thriving* individual means you are growing and developing well. Thriving individuals live well-balanced, fulfilled lives, really doing what they like with love, passion, and whole lot of self-respect and dignity.

Thriving means growing and developing well, as in, "the new baby thrived." We want to think of ourselves as the baby, thriving daily. Other definitions are to make steady progress and/or to prosper.[8] Every individual wants to prosper, but only by focusing on your goals and making little but firm steps toward them can we make it.

The difference between being a survivor vs. identifying yourself as a thriving individual is that as a thriving individual, you are conscious of who you are; you have accepted yourself entirely; and you are OK with that. You are OK with the good, the so-called bad, the so-so, and it is all perfectly fine. You know you are thriving when:

- You are OK speaking in terms of your truth.
- You can say *no* without feeling guilty.
- You say your true feelings without being scared of the opinion of others.
- You do not need to prove yourself to anyone, only to yourself.
- You live at peace with yourself, and/or within your world or within any storm.

---

[8] . "Thrive," Merriam-Webster Dictionary, https://www.merriam-webster.com/dictionary/thrive.

When you can enjoy your own company without the need for a multitude of people, then you aren't just thriving, you are living in awe. Life everywhere—in Italy, in the streets with the homeless, in the company of your best friend—is your home. You are at home in any circumstance, and nothing will be out of place. You will be kind, especially to the person who matters most: yourself.

At this point, you are being the best that you can be, and you are extremely excited because you know more lies ahead. Every experience, even the stormy nights, is an opportunity to learn and grow. You are not afraid because you know that any new experience that comes your way, good or bad, you will learn from and move on. At this point, stagnation will have a new meaning, knowing that even during this time, you can learn to be a better human being.

Being a thriving individual is living, really experiencing life, one punch at a time, and totally enjoying it. It does not mean that you know everything, not really. It just means you know the most important of all things, *you*, and you can depend on that.

Now it is important that you, if not already, continue to reflect on your point of identification. Identify in which of these phases you think you may be and if you have ever thought about any of this. It is important that you are truly honest with yourself and know that what you're embarking on will move you away from your comfort zone. It may leave you naked to yourself and, what is most scary, to the world. Up to now, you have been a victim of something terrible and have done your best to survive. However, you probably want to move beyond this … right?

What is your comfort zone? We always silently want something to change, hoping that our lives can be different. However, most of the time, we do nothing about it. Thus, most of the time we stay stuck on that wish. Have you ever asked yourself why?

Perhaps it is all interrelated. It could be part of our self-imposed limitations—our thoughts that we are not good enough for that job, that person, and that house—combined with the fear of change: *Well, if I leave this job where I know everyone and I make good money, how will I find another job where I can maybe get paid more, travel more, etc.? How will I feel in a new city far from my friends and family? Who will I talk to if I let go of the only friend I have, even though I know this friend does not act in my best interest? How can I break off this relationship with this person who most of the time neglects me?* So, we stay in a dead marriage or dead-end job, and we continue to deal with toxic family and friends we know we should have distanced ourselves from years ago.

The fact is that change is scary, as it involves the unknown. But even when we are doing all we can for there not to be any change, it happens without our consent—such as when illness comes our way, we are laid off, the person we thought would be with us forever has taken a liking to someone else, or our now-adult child goes to another state and leaves us empty-nested. What then? Opening the door to change and understanding that it is inevitable may assist you in welcoming it—and in that welcoming can come what you have been waiting for, the change you have always wanted. Thus, the need for self-reflecting, as in that process you can ease the fear of transitioning to the change you have always desired.

Before we move on, know that there will be a few side effects that will come from your identifying process. You will be calmer, yet with a new organic and unlimited energy that people will be wondering where you are getting it from. You will become a person with confidence, with great esteem for yourself that will not allow you to engage in unnecessary bickering, violence, or unwanted situations. It will encourage you to set long forgotten boundaries, allowing you to leave certain people or situations out of your life.

Setting boundaries is a huge side effect to watch for, and one that can bring much pain and division, even between family members. However, at the end of it, setting boundaries will leave you with many unforeseen fruits and a new beginning you may never have thought possible. It is often common in enmeshed family homes that even after years of sexual abuse, the abuser is part of the family and perhaps has abused others. Because sexual abuse is so complex, the raising of voices within homes is censored. The elephant in the room is ignored, and life continues as we condone this behavior and allow for more abuse.

Setting boundaries can be liberating, yet it takes a whole lot of courage. We are used to our masks and the rationale behind their use.

Changing course is frightening. But it allows you to see individuals in a different light and allow them to be at their own level, without judgment. You will become loving even to those who may question your kindness. You will walk away from negative situations quietly and without fuss.

You will love more and care more, but without the fear of being hurt. Being vulnerable will be OK and even welcomed at times. You will understand why some roads must close and some must open. You will learn to live within the current and not against it. You will learn to indulge in fear and come out fearless—or come out with fear but out indeed! You will be you and be OK with that. You will learn to let go of individuals, even family members, who have and still hurt you because of your courage to address the elephant in the room.

Having been a victim of sexual abuse greatly increases the chances that you will tolerate toxic people in your life. Thus, you need to reflect and be conscious of the importance of keeping this type of individual at a fairly healthy distance. The person who abused you was a toxic person—a person who caused you harm, who did not respect your rights as a human being and left you confused and vulnerable. As the meaning of *toxic* indicates, this person added negativity and destruction to your life.

Perhaps other toxic individuals can't possibly compare to this individual, but in their own way, they can keep you from reaching your full potential. This is done in many ways, including:

- lies
- inability to respect your boundaries
- different ways to manipulate you into doing what they want
- always leaving you confused and questioning yourself
- negative remarks
- straightforward put-downs.

Bullying is a subtle and perhaps inconspicuous act that can, without notice, keep you from being open and forthcoming to the changes you may so desire.

At this stage, you will be able to start separating the toxic people from the rest. Be wary of the changes that come, as they will take you to a space of freedom that you may have never experienced before, leaving you in a complete state of awe but at times with a bit of what many may consider loneliness. However, know that this loneliness is what allows you to come closer to the person who matters the most: *you*.

EXERCISE

Create an imaginary maze like the one in the Pac-Man game. In the maze, the blue whale, representing the thriver, is the one on a quest. The victim is represented by a baby elephant, the survivor by a sea turtle, the accomplisher by a sea horse, and the striver by a Japanese puffer fish. Upon successfully identifying and moving through these phases, represented by the blue whale eating them, the thriver is left to enjoy the fruits of thriving. Having consumed the victim, the survivor, the striver, and the accomplisher, the thriver (blue whale) accumulates points and finally become its thriving image.

CHAPTER 2

COMMON HIDEOUTS

Experiencing abuse in any form during the formative years can be a challenge to overcome for any individual. Imagine being sexually abused by a caregiver, friend, or relative who, as a child, you depended on for love, support, nurture, trust, and security. Most victims of sexual abuse experience a general sense of disgust, shame, and/or anger coupled with the physical and spiritual aspect of it. Know that not one of these effects ever really comes alone. It is usually a combination of all and then some.

Guilt is one feeling that in particular can take a toll on a person if not appropriately addressed. Thus, it is important to review the meaning of words and know your basic rights as a human being, and how those were so utterly violated. Many changes in your personality and behavior— unconsciously and, much less frequently, consciously—take effect. It is like a melting pot where many emotions, thoughts, and irrational ideas about life and people come together. These long- and short-term effects impact you in school, work, and social events, in your intrapersonal and interpersonal relationships, for the rest of your being in this world.

GUILT

Before moving on to some common defense mechanisms, let's explore the feeling of guilt. Words with similar meanings to *guilt* include *ashamed, responsible*, and *sinful*. Although those considered victims should not feel any sense of guilt, as they have not and did not do anything to deserve this kind of treatment, the mind and feelings these individuals may hold toward the perpetrator can indeed cause feelings of guilt.

Age can be another factor that contributes to how individuals process incidents and/or traumas in their life. For example, those younger than eight will not be able to process information in the same way as a person at thirty. Children will not have the resources to understand that they do not hold any kind of responsibility for the actions of others. For example, children are much more concrete in their thinking and may explain a spanking from a parent as a consequence of them not being good. They will do anything to be the good child and get the attention needed from their loved one. If this is not adequately processed or explained, these individuals will have the false belief that *I always have to be good to be loved* and put aside their real feelings just to feel loved by their caretakers.

With this said, many feelings or personal desires when displayed or felt can give a sense of guilt. Feelings of guilt can develop in many traumatic or non-traumatic scenes of their life and can be devastating, taking that person down the road to self-destruction.

Another scenario can be that after children disclose to someone what is happening to them, that person makes a report to the police, and the abuser—let's say the father—is arrested. At this time, children will feel guilty and responsible, as because of their disclosure, their father is now in custody and unable to provide for the family. It happens that the father is the main breadwinner in the home. Additionally, some relatives are unable to believe what this individual has done, and so the victim becomes the oddball and the one to blame. There are many more scenarios in which the individual accepts blame for the abuse without really being the one to blame.

Because our minds are tricky in their processes, we need to continually educate ourselves and self-reflect. Feelings of guilt can take many to the grave before their time, especially when exposed at such a young age, when problem-solving resources are limited. Thus, we need to theoretically carve up this topic until nothing is left unsaid, and reflection and awareness are part of our daily bread.

DEFENSE MECHANISMS

Sigmund Freud was a famous psychiatrist from the late 1800s and is responsible for defining the most common defense mechanisms that individuals develop to deal with or function under different traumas or negative experiences, consciously and/or unconsciously, when unable to deal with issues too burdensome to comprehend at the time of the incident. Freud was best known for developing the theories and techniques of psychoanalysis. One key feature of psychoanalysis is that it understands how our behavior is closely related to our unconscious and conscious thoughts, which mainly stem from our inability to understand or accept different traumatic experiences.

Children who are sexually violated by an adult who is supposed to be taking care of them will have many emotional and cognitive distortions and/or irrational beliefs about themselves, people, and society in general. Some examples of cognitive distortions include:

- poor emotional reasoning
- catastrophizing and/or minimizing events
- problems filtering information
- assuming one is always right
- assuming something will turn out badly

It is unavoidable that after experiencing such an ordeal, a person will develop defense mechanisms to cope most of the time unconsciously, with the traumatic event at hand.

The following are the most talked-about defense mechanisms introduced by Sigmund Freud and later expanded on by his daughter Anna Freud that individuals may use, either consciously or unconsciously, to protect themselves from traumatic experiences. I find that reviewing the definitions of these defense mechanisms and reflecting on whether you have used and still are using them can be a key factor in helping you to question and understand your actions until now. Maybe at this point of identification, you start to realize that you have been in either fight or flight mode, and you have not truly had the time to learn about your experiences, assisting you to become more in tune with who you truly are.

DEFENSE MECHANISMS

Definitions for the following defense mechanisms have been taken from *The Social Work Dictionary* by Robert L. Baker.[9]

Repression

Repression is a defense mechanism whereby the individual unconsciously pushes out of the conscious mind certain memories, ideas, or desires that are unacceptable or cause a high level of anxiety. However, even though these memories are now contained in the unconscious mind, they may come out in behavior in disguised forms. This defense mechanism helps you to temporarily continue to function within your environment but are not healthy coping strategies.

For example, a person who has used repression or has hidden away abuse in his subconscious may have ongoing and unresolved issues that arise in different ways. People who were sexually abused by a male parent who they depended on as a child may later in life have difficulty trusting and forming healthy relationships, especially with male authority figures at work, and not be conscious of the reason for this. Nonetheless, they can function within their immediate environment. Thus, they will continue to repress any painful memory of abuse.

Suppression

In suppression, your conscious mind is rejecting unpleasant thoughts. Suppression is like repression, but in suppression, you are consciously deciding not to think about what you went through to

---

[9] . Robert L. Barker, *The Social Work Dictionary*, 5th reprint ed. (Washington, DC: NASW Press, 2003).

protect yourself from harmful feelings like disgust, shame, sadness, and the insecurities this brings.

For example, people who have been sexually abused as a child by a male parent purposely avoid male authority figures who remind them of the incident. Compared to repression, suppression may be healthier, as you are more aware; yet only in the short run. Eventually, this may keep you from establishing and/or meeting wonderful individuals who have not and will never really harm you.

Denial

Denial is the defense mechanism that protects the individual from anxiety or guilt by ignoring unacceptable thoughts, emotions, or wishes. In denial, you are not accepting that something is happening. Denying that you were abused sexually as a child and not understanding and/ or accepting that this may have brought many cognitive distortions or irrational beliefs will indeed prolong your healing process. It will keep you from consciously focusing on other things, such as having healthier relationships, trusting, and loving yourself for who you are and what you represent.

Displacement

Displacement is a defense mechanism used to reduce anxiety. It deals with certain thoughts, feelings, or wishes by unconsciously shifting them to other thoughts, feelings, persons, or wishes that are more acceptable or tolerable. For example: People who were sexually abused by a male parent who they depended on may have never been able to confront that parent and express their own feelings of anger. Therefore, they can unconsciously displace that anger onto other male figures close to them, to their own son, or to any other male among family or friends who is less harmful and therefore a safer target (someone who more than likely will not retaliate or confront them). Displacement, although it works, can bring devastating relational experiences, keeping you from forming trusting and fulfilling relationships with those who matter the most, such as your child, friends, and family.

Rationalization

Rationalization involves presenting in logical terms, or interpreting the reasons for, some action or event. It is also defined as a defense mechanism in which a person explains or justifies an action or thought to make it acceptable when, at a deeper psychological level, it is unacceptable.

For example, people who have been sexually abused as a child by a male parent they depended on for love and support will be emotionally torn between feelings of anger and love and may rationalize what happened to them as, "This would not have happened to me if I had not talked back to him and gotten him so upset. I am a bad person," or "He does this because he loves me." This may be a way to condone someone's inappropriate behavior, which can leave the door open for more abuse and revictimization, and leave you always attempting to explain others' behaviors toward you. This may well be detrimental to your mental health and leave you more vulnerable to abuse, and, as a result, it is one to watch for.

To further understand defense mechanisms, you may want to look at the video by Lewis Psychology, 7 Freudian Defense Mechanism Explained (https://www.youtube.com/watch?v=fTnjJ105ze4), in where defense mechanisms are further explained. [10]

KNOWING YOUR DEFENSE MECHANISMS

It is likely that you have unconsciously and/or consciously used these defense mechanisms to cope with trauma, and at times of crisis, we definitely should be thankful for our natural tendencies to use them and get into survival mode. Using these defense mechanisms

---

[10] . Lewis Psychology: 7 Freudian Defense Mechanism Explained, November 17, 2018, https://www.youtube.com/watch?v=fTnjJ105ze4

will temporarily serve us, as we need to keep on functioning despite our experiences. However, if left undealt with, they can leave us with devastating effects in the long run. It will be beneficial to become familiar with them, as it will give you insight into how you have dealt with and continue to deal with trauma and/or negative events in your life, including sexual abuse.

Knowing your defense mechanisms will enable you to evaluate whether they continue to be the healthiest way to cope with traumatic events in your life. It will also help you in the process of becoming aware that there may be internal scars you have still to confront to finally understand that you are no different from anyone, in the sense that abuse is abuse no matter how you look at it.

This takes us back to the first step: knowing you were a victim and understanding that you were violated physically, emotionally, and yes, spiritually too. You were a victim violated in many ways at an early age, leaving you with gaps in your developmental process for which, unconsciously or consciously, you naturally resorted to using any one of these defense mechanisms to continue to function at that point in time and have been doing so up to now.

There have been other defense mechanisms described by other professionals since Freud; however, I have found his to be in common use with those experiencing trauma during my years of practice. Acknowledge whether you too have used some of Freud's main defense mechanisms to function and/or survive. If you recognize that you are still using these defense mechanisms, as most of us have done during different periods of our lives, you are still in Phase 2: The Survivor.

What are our basic rights? What were your basic rights the moment you were born? I find that reviewing our basic human rights helps us to reflect deeper and see exactly how much we were violated to utterly understand how we were at one time victimized. This is fundamental to the healing process.

From the moment a child is born, what are that individual's basic rights? Sometime in 1945, after World War II, "The Universal Declaration of Human Rights" was produced—with the help of a great First Lady, Mrs. Eleanor Roosevelt, who referred to it as the

"International Magna Carta for All Mankind."[11] From the thirty or so articles in the document, I found that article 1 described well the rights of all human beings, including children:

> All human beings are born free and equal in dignity and rights. They are endowed with reason and conscience and should act towards one another in a spirit of brotherhood.

To understand this article, let's go a bit further and ask, "What is brotherhood?"

Brotherhood is defined as "the belief that all people should act with warmth and equality toward one another."[12] I add and emphasize the word *respect*. We should all act with respect toward one another, as I believe that respect encompasses it all: warmth, love, and equality. If I do not respect you, more than likely, I do not hold you in regard. If I hold you in regard, I respect you, and therefore I will more than likely treat you with warmth and equality. But then what we should make sure of is that this includes all humankind, especially young children, the elderly, and vulnerable adults, as they too have something to contribute to our society. By this, we are practicing true brotherhood.

At the end of it all, what you need to understand is that yes, your basic rights as a human being, as written under the Universal Declaration of Human Rights, were plainly and simply taken away. The person who violated you did not, obviously, act toward you in a spirit of brotherhood. Thus, in the time that you depended upon an adult to protect and love you, you were violated. You became a victim, a person who was cheated out of being treated with the dignity and respect you are entitled to from the moment you are born.

---

11 . "The Universal Declaration of Human Rights, UDHR, Declaration of Human Rights, Human Rights Declaration, Human Rights Charter, The UN, and Human Rights," *UN News Center*, November 9, 2014, web. https://www.un.org/en/about-us/universal-declaration-of-human-rights

12 . "Brotherhood," Collins English Dictionary, https://www.collinsdictionary.com/dictionary/english/brotherhood.

The person who cared for you did not act toward you in a spirit of brotherhood. There is no need to justify yourself or their behavior, let alone have feelings of shame, doubt, or guilt. You were a victim of a horrible crime, and now you will need to come to grips with it. Failure to accept, understand, and help yourself will cause you to re-victimize yourself repeatedly.

Re-victimizing yourself happens when you continue to feel shame, disgust, sadness, and repulsion, and when you repeatedly act as if nothing happened, when you are stuck not being yourself and when you continue to let silence lead the way. You need to lead the way instead of allowing the experiences you have had in the past, such as having been sexually abused as a child, lead the way.

Think about the child within you who is still hurting and accept that your basic rights as a human being were taken away. To some degree, you have avoided or violated your *own* rights by not allowing yourself to understand and/or accept the abuse you have endured. For instance, a seven-year-old boy stripped of his innocence has continued to violate his own rights if, by the age of forty, he continues to feel guilt, rationalize, or suppress his feelings, and is unable to consciously accept that he was a victim of sexual abuse. At age forty, he still disregards his own voice completely.

Your mission should be to regain your voice and have an unclouded vision of your basic human rights and respect for those rights at all times. Your rights should be respected and cherished by you and those around you in a healthy and appropriate manner in accordance with society. Once you are able to internalize the violation of your basic rights as a human being, it will become easier to exit from those feelings of guilt and shame and put the responsibility for such violations on those directly and indirectly responsible. Then will come your true freedom.

With your rights in mind, I want to show you a simple mathematical way to assist yourself in the identifying process, which will also help whenever you are confronted with a lingering problem. I call it Math Psychology. Do the math with me.

MATH PSYCHOLOGY, PART 1

Ask yourself in simple mathematical terms: How many years did the abuse take place? When did it start? How old are you now? Let's say that the abuse started taking place when you were four, and it lasted until age twelve. Right now, you are forty years old.

If you subtract four from twelve, unfortunately, you had to experience this abuse for eight long years. And now if you subtract from the time the abuse stopped from your current age, twelve from forty equals twenty-eight. So you have a total of twenty-eight years that either consciously or unconsciously, you have been re-victimizing yourself with feelings of shame, disgust, guilt, poor self-concept, low self-esteem, and all that comes with them.

Just think about it and stop whatever you are doing right now. Twenty-eight years have passed since the actual abuse took place, yet it is there, subconsciously, taking place daily. Yes, you have managed to survive and function for twenty-eight years. However, ask yourself if that experience is still affecting you, and be as honest with yourself as possible. Now compare eight years to twenty-eight years and ask yourself, *How long will I let this, and any other experience, run my life?* What will happen ten years, twenty years, or thirty years from now?

Visualize these different age groups: forty through fifty, fifty through sixty, and yes, even seventy through eighty, and ask yourself the following questions:

- Where will I be ten years from now?
- Where would I like to be?
- What would I like to accomplish?
- What are my dreams?
- Am I where I want to be now?
- How will I help myself reach my goals, daily?
- How well do I cope with different traumatic situations in my life?
- What are my main defense mechanisms and how have they helped or not helped?

- What is my overall behavior when confronted with change in my life?
- Who will be there to support me, and who is there right now?
- Where can I go for help if I need it?

Consider your answers and ask yourself the most important question of all: *For how many more years will I let my experience with child sexual abuse or rape affect my overall quality of life? Why do I need to continue granting so much power to the evil spirit that tried to destroy my life? Why?*

MATH PSYCHOLOGY, PART 2

Part 2 takes you further to ask, to what age do you expect to live? Let's suppose you expect to live until you are eighty years old, and right now you are only forty.

OK, simple! You subtract forty from eighty, equaling forty. You have approximately forty years left until you are eighty. What will you do in those forty years?

This simple math calculation can give you a vision, lead you to logical and factual reasoning, and allow you to readily problem-solve (depending on the time you have to waste). It may open the door to many other questions, such as: *What quality of life do I want to have for the remaining forty years?* It can help you turn it all around and transform the suffering and re-victimizing of yourself to count as something meaningful and positive in your life. Was this abuse or any kind of trauma, no matter how traumatic, worth you living in the depths of despair and your own revictimization for forty more years?

You will turn an experience that almost destroyed you to one that will leave you with immeasurable benefits in your life. Will the next forty years be a resemblance of *you* leading the way, or will it resemble the aftermath of abuse or trauma? Ask yourself repeatedly: Why would you give those who harmed you your power, your love, your spirit, your humanity, and for so long? Why would you give this experience forty more years of suffering without having the necessary courage to confront it? Dr. Steve Maraboli suggests, "Free yourself from the burden of a past you cannot change."[13]

SELF-AWARENESS QUESTIONNAIRE

To help you in doing your math psychology, take this self-awareness questionnaire and dare to be as honest as possible. To have self-awareness/self-reflection or to self-clean, consider your responses to the questions below. It is essential in the healing process to accept who you are and to start letting go of so much pain.

When did the abuse start?

_____

_____

_____

_____

_____

How old are you now?

_____

_____

_____

_____

_____

13 . "Steve Maraboli Quotes," Goodreads, https://www.goodreads.com/quotes/1289557-let-go-how-would-your-life-be-different-if-you.

How many years has this experience consciously or unconsciously affected you? (Use Math Psychology, Part 1, on the previous page and refer back to the information on defense mechanisms).

_____

_____

_____

_____

_____

_____

_____

_____

_____

Are you where you want to be right now?

_____

_____

_____

_____

_____

_____

_____

_____

_____

_____

Will you continue granting so much power to the situation that has put limitations on and possibly destroyed your life and has the potential to keep you stagnant in the past?

_____

_____

_____

_____

_____

_____

_____

_____

_____

How would you like to see yourself in ten, twenty, thirty years?

_____

_____

_____

_____

_____

_____

_____

To what age would you like to live?

_____

_____

What are some goals you would like to accomplish? (Start with at least one attainable objective.)

_____

_____

_____

_____

_____

_____

_____

_____

_____

What are your dreams?

_____

_____

_____

_____

_____

_____

_____

_____

_____

What do you plan to do daily to help yourself reach these goals?

_____

_____

_____

_____

_____

_____

_____

What are your mind tricks? (These will be further discussed in chapter 9.)

_____

_____

_____

_____

_____

_____

_____

_____

_____

How well do you cope with different traumatic situations in your life now? Is the glass half full or half empty?

_____

_____

_____

_____

_____

_____

_____

_____

_____

What main defense mechanism have you unconsciously/consciously been using to cope?

_____

_____

_____

_____

_____

_____

_____

_____

In reference to the defense mechanisms used: Have they been helpful in the short run? What about in the long run?

_____

_____

_____

_____

_____

_____

_____

_____

_____

_____

Have you noticed your behavior when confronted with change in your life?

_____

_____

_____

_____

_____

_____

_____

_____

_____

How do you react to change? (hostility, anxiety, confrontation, depression, etc.)

_____

_____

_____

_____

_____

_____

_____

_____

Who do you go to for support?

_____

_____

_____

_____

_____

Do you trust anyone, truly?

_____

_____

_____

_____

_____

For how many more years will you let your experience of child sexual abuse/sexual abuse affect your overall quality of life? (See Math Psychology, Part 2.)

_____

_____

_____

_____

_____

_____

_____

_____

_____

Why would you give those who harmed you your power, your love, your spirit, your humanity, and for so long? Why? (See Math Psychology, Part 2.)

_____

_____

_____

_____

_____

_____

_____

_____

How do you relate to others/peers/family/friends?

_____

_____

_____

_____

_____

_____

_____

_____

_____

_____

What is your tolerance level for abuse?

_____

_____

_____

_____

_____

_____

_____

_____

_____

Write as much as you can in the provided spaces, and be aware that writing can serve as another tool to help you come to terms with your abuse.

Often, professionals recommend journaling, and I can only emphasize the power that writing something down can have on you and how it can help you deal with any present situation as well as in your healing process. Remember that afterward, you can rip that paper into very little, little pieces. Just the process of writing and visualizing your feelings and events on paper can have a significant impact on your life.

Take, for example, *The Diary of Anne Frank*, started by Anne within the secret annex where she wrote for two years about her feelings and events that took place, describing each of the individuals hiding in the annex during the Holocaust. She named her diary Kitty, and Kitty helped her deal with this devastating situation where there was so much sadness and despair. Kitty helped transform it to beauty, where it was possible to hope.

I have read this diary more than twice, and every time, I felt the depth of this experience; but also, I see beauty. Perhaps she was not aware, but she transcended with hope and love, and during those two years she was able to cope and live each day as the last day, giving her all, and she was only thirteen to fifteen years old.

As a result, Anne lived on and is known for her wonderful writing abilities, her love for humanity, and her own personal experience with the secret annex. Thus, writing down on a paper your trauma, your feelings, and your goals can have significant resonance in your life. Try it!

Do the math.

CHAPTER 3
SEXUAL ABUSE: IMPACTS OVER TIME

The focus in this chapter is for you to know about the long-term effects of sexual abuse with a brief overview of the grooming process. The grooming process can easily resemble the techniques used by a hunter when attempting to catch its prey. The hunter, or in this case, the perpetrator, will set traps and even paint his face and wear clothes that camouflage his real self or his presence from his prey. He will more likely deceive his targeted prey, as well as those within the prey's immediate environment.

Becoming aware of the long-term effects of sexual abuse and their presence in your life can serve as another tool to help you further internalize the need to continue on your path toward thriving. Unfortunately, the long-term effects of sexual abuse can be devastating, with the potential for unwanted endings, such as is suicide.

When children, male or female, are sexually abused during their developmental stages, they are left with many gaps and develop many defense mechanisms, as previously discussed. These gaps in their developmental stages will impact them well into adulthood, leaving the individual prone to higher and more chronic physical ailments (poor overall health), psychological ailments (depression, anxiety, PTSD), and behavioral difficulties (such as substance abuse).[14] In addition,

---

[14] . "Fast Facts: Preventing Child Sexual Abuse," Violence Prevention, Centers for Disease Control and Prevention (CDC), accessed October 30, 2022, https://www.cdc.gov/violenceprevention/childsexualabuse/fastfact.html.

psychosocial problems (prone to have interpersonal problems/divorce), socioeconomic problems, and diminished cognitive skills will also be evident.

Several resources agree on the following most common[15] long-term effects of childhood sexual abuse:

- low self-esteem, feelings of self-hatred or shame
- an inability to trust, often leading to difficulties in establishing relationships
- sexual difficulties or a lack of ability to feel sexual with individuals other than those with whom there is no attachment
- continuation of the sexual-abuse cycle: marrying an abusive partner or abusing one's own children
- increase in alcohol or drug use, sometimes leading to substance abuse disorders
- chronic abdominal, urinary tract, or gynecological problems
- repressed anger and hostility
- depression and thoughts of suicide
- anxiety and panic disorders
- eating disorders such as anorexia nervosa; an obsessive concern about food, weight, and body image that leads to self-starvation; or bulimia, the destructive cycle of binge eating and purging.
- dissociative disorders, the most severe form being multiple personality disorder, now under dissociative disorders in the DSM-5
- "damaged goods" syndrome: a negative body image due to self-blame
- sexual difficulties such as fear of sex or intimacy, indiscriminate multiple sex partners, or difficulty in reaching orgasm
- parenting problems, such as fear of being a bad parent, of abusing the child, or of being overprotective (part of poor interpersonal skills)
- flashbacks and/or panic attacks

---

[15] . RAINN's Corporate Partners, "Effects of Sexual Violence," revised 2023, https://rainn.org/effects-sexual-violence?_ga=2.73149654.454341927.1683996650-1052821332.1683996650.

THE GROOMING PROCESS

To further understand the so-called "grooming process," and to possibly help in prevention, it is important to know the most common tactics used by the perpetrator. These may deceive not only the child and/or adult targeted for the abuse but also those who are responsible for protecting the child and/or vulnerable adult. These are resources that may ultimately function to keep sexual abuse out of your home, school, community, etc.

Grooming tactics can be used by perpetrators to get the targeted potential victim and those around the potential victim to trust them and eventually put them in control of the situation, giving abusers an open door. When abusers are in control, they can do as they wish without suspecting adults to worry about. The abuser is left to manipulate the victim into succumbing to any sexual act desired by the abuser and persuades the child to secrecy. Secrecy usually happens and continues for longer periods of time when abusers manipulate victims into thinking that either no one cares about them or the abuser will hurt them if they say anything.

There are an infinite number of ways an abuser can manipulate the victim to remain quiet, but what allows the abuser to be successful in continuing the abuse is the inability of those around the victim to become aware of what may be going on. Therefore, the urgent need to become more vigilant (not paranoid) at recognizing the grooming process.

SIX STAGES OF GROOMING

Taken from "Grooming" on the website of Mothers of Sexually Abused Children (MOSAC).[16]

1. Targeting the victim
2. Gaining the victim's trust: they try to be extra special to the child, try to fulfill all of child's needs.

---

[16] . Retrieved October 30, 2022, https://www.mosac.net/page/46.

3. Filling a need (filling a need the child may have in any area, especially any lack of emotional support from the main caregivers)
4. Isolating the child
5. Sexualizing the relationship
6. Maintaining control

When is the grooming process for the abuser easiest? It is good to remember that victims are targeted by their perpetrator 99 percent of time way before the grooming process starts. In addition, remember that 90 percent of the time, the perpetrator is a family member.

Like a hunter, perpetrators will single out their prey easily if they notice some type of lack in a victim's life—for instance, when they can observe that children are being neglected by the responsible adults around them; being left home alone due to inability to pay a sitter; emotionally or physically deprived, and/or lacking material things.

For example, children who are left home alone often due to their parents' need to work may be an easy target, as they may need that bond with and attention from an adult. While, at the same time, parents need for a trusted babysitter can take precedence. Perpetrators may see the parents' needs and the child's lack of attention as an opportunity, where they can come in and offer just what the family is lacking in an attempt to get the trust needed to increase the possibility of being around the designated victim.

There are many other scenarios in which it is easy for a child to fall prey. In any case, the preparator will offer what is lacking, such as trust, affection, and money. Once the victim trusts, the abuser will move from nonsexual touch to sexual touch, leading the victim to allow more sexual or physical encounters.

More examples of grooming techniques described by MOSAC are:

- giving bribes, gifts, special privileges, excessive compliments
- being too affectionate (hugging, holding hands, rubbing back, inappropriate kissing)
- pretending to wrestle
- sharing common interests with the victim

- taking the victim to a secluded place
- threats and intimidation to victim, pet, family member, or friend
- convincing the victim by pretending that sex is a game
- using a position of authority or blackmail
- use of pornography to sexualize child

Reviewing the grooming process is part of the plan of this guide for you to self-reflect and see how, in so many ways, you were deceived, used, and manipulated by an individual at an age at which you had absolutely no tools to keep yourself safe and were completely dependent on those around you for protection and love. Knowing about this grooming process also allows you to compartmentalize in your mind those responsible or not for your abuse, again putting the responsibility for such a crime in the hands of those who committed it, not you.

Inform yourself as much as possible and be aware that you are never alone in the journey to persevere, despite any circumstance you find yourself in. Remember that there is always a positive way out of any situation. In life, there is good and bad; it is just that the bad, unfortunately, is emphasized more in our world. Be aware of how and what constitutes child sexual abuse and how it continues to be a broad social problem. You will find later, in chapter 5, the statistics of how common sexual abuse is and some generalizations about perpetrators.

Unfortunately, there are millions of individuals who have experienced child sexual abuse and still struggle daily with their silence. And then there are others, not as fortunate as you, who may never have the opportunity to help themselves break the cycle of years of revictimization, who will walk this earth with their tails tucked between their legs, punishing and blaming themselves for something they had no control over and was not their fault, unable to seek the help needed—as you have and *will*. Many who are not able to recognize the devastating effects that come from falling victim to sexual abuse may find temporary or permanent solutions in suicide, substance abuse, or other addictions that will consume their life. Thus, continue to inform yourself. Ask, ask, ask!

CHAPTER 4

ASK, ASK, ASK!

O nce you are thoroughly aware of the person you are, knowledgeable decisions can be made. Think about it: how can you decide on who will be a good partner for you, when to have children, or what career to pursue if you don't know who you are? By learning who you are, you allow yourself to open new doors that may offer a new and fresh perspective on life.

Understanding who you are will allow you to make better decisions and help you find quicker solutions when faced with life challenges. This is the moment when you should start questioning, asking, and doubting all that you hear and see, and analyzing those around you who you believe have overcome many obstacles to become thriving individuals. This is the moment when you start reducing that unreachable mountain your mind has placed between you and your dreams, allowing your mind frame to change from impossible to possible. Look around. Observe those you identify as successful people. Analyze and question everyone and everything.

If you ever have the chance or have gone to Walt Disney World, stop for a moment and ask yourself: How did all this creativity come to be? How did the idea begin? How did Walt Disney go beyond his limits, and how did he manage to thrive even after having to overcome his personal struggles? Remember that all individuals are faced with trauma in their lifetime that needs to be confronted before they can become who they were meant to be.

Your biggest challenge is to confront that the fact that you were abused as a child and your rights were violated. You need to come to terms with that. Others may have to confront different situations, such as growing up as an abandoned child, losing a job, divorce, or postpartum depression. Whatever the case, the issue must be confronted, accepted, and worked through before you can become who you were truly meant to be.

Every individual has a story. Every individual has faced or will face a dilemma, and it may not necessarily be one as traumatic as being sexually abused in your formative years. However, you are the one who decides how a dilemma will make or break you.

If people are not conscious of the devastating effects that come from a traumatic experience, it may cripple them. Their inability to see beyond an experience, such as being sexually abused, and constant tendency toward self-revictimization may well go on for the rest of their being, keeping them from finding their true purpose, freedom, or even their essence. As I have emphasized repeatedly, it is imperative that you become aware of your own coping styles, cognitive distortions, and conscious or unconscious use of defense mechanisms (as described in chapter 2).

On your journey to search within, I want to explain to you how creating the habit of "Ask, ask, ask" can help you become aware of your own coping styles and your cognitive distortions. You will be surprised to learn that things do not just happen by chance. This will awaken you to the fact that behind the scenes of every success story is struggle, tears, self-doubt, and in one way or the other, the overcoming of a traumatic experience.

Ask: How do some people, despite their broken childhoods, adolescence, or even adulthood, continue to pursue their innermost dreams? Ask: How do some people keep going despite their seen and unseen limitations? Ask: How can they push boundaries to ultimately accomplish that which seemed impossible given their upbringing and/or their circumstances?

For this guide, when I refer to *asking*, it means to engage yourself in questioning, observing, analyzing, inquiring, and researching how individuals, including those who have passed away, continued to persevere despite their traumatic experience. *Asking* is being curious enough to find out that there are people who, despite the odds, make it and are successful. Despite the odds, they find their success. They become an image of the thriving individual they were always meant to be, and those are the people who are living and not merely surviving. Think about all those who, despite their own dilemmas, have transitioned into what I call "thriving individuals." This is your goal!

This is the moment where I must emphasize the importance of *asking.* However, when inquiring, it is good to remember that everyone is different, and a traumatic experience is defined by the individual. For instance, a divorce may be a traumatic experience for you but not necessarily for Kerry, who was ready to get a divorce after the first week of marriage. And what about Sandy, who was raised by a single mother with an absent father, who felt this situation was traumatic and difficult to overcome, versus Anne, who was perfectly fine being raised by her single mother and absent father, yet defined the loss of her business as a traumatic experience. As the saying goes, there are different strokes for different folks. What is traumatic for you may not be so for another person.

What is important is not how you define your experience but how you confront it. That will make all the difference, and it will determine the outcome. The process of *asking* will help you discover that each person who has gone beyond to become a thriving individual has at one point faced one or more traumatic experiences. Briefly, it is not the traumatic experience per se but how you choose to deal with it that will set the stage for change and growth.

In your mission toward finding *you*, during the *asking* phase, imagine yourself in a classroom completing an experiment, and the result of your experiment turns out completely different from what you had hypothesized. What happens then? At this moment, you begin to question and analyze how and why this happened.

This scenario describes someone being exposed to the cognitive learning strategies devised by Dr. Benjamin Bloom. This cognitive learning process, called Bloom's taxonomy, takes us to the idea of asking the right questions to ensure effective learning. This is your main goal in this chapter and in your daily existence: to remain curious and question *everything*.

Beth Lewis, an elementary education expert, refers to Bloom's taxonomy as a "hierarchy of question stems that teachers use to guide their students through the learning process."[17] For example, "When students are first being introduced to a new topic, teachers use Bloom's Taxonomy to get ideas for basic questions that ask the students to recall simple facts from the material. As students' comprehension grows and evolves, the questions will get more complex and demand more from the students."

In Bloom's revised taxonomy, the pyramid of thinking starts with the basic steps of remembering, then understanding, applying, analyzing, evaluating, to ultimately create. Bloom's taxonomy is used by teachers to assist students in building the ability to answer more complex questions by starting with the basics as indicated above (remembering, understanding, applying, analyzing, evaluating, and ultimately creating). By using his method, the teacher is providing the basic steps to help students eventually reach the point where they develop the habit of more complex thinking, which may lead them to create. This ability to create can be viewed as parallel to your ability to identify yourself as *the thriver* in the find-the-way steps. Identify what step you are on in Bloom's taxonomy, starting with the basic steps of remembering, which entail identifying and/or labeling your immediate knowledge. In this way, you engage in critical thinking. Critically analyzing what step you are in is the basic step toward building the foundation to the better *thriving* you, the creator you.[18]

If you incorporate the basic ideas presented in the Bloom's taxonomy cognitive learning process to your situation and recognize the connection to my find-the-way steps (to review steps, refer to chapter 1), you will

---

[17] . Beth Lewis, "Using Bloom's Taxonomy for Effective Learning," ThoughtCo, November 10, 2019, https://www.thoughtco.com/blooms-taxonomy-the-incredible-teaching-tool2081869.

[18] . Heather Coffey, "Bloom's Taxonomy," 2008, https://www.researchgate.net/profile/Heather-Coffey/publication/242546164_Bloom%27s_Taxonomy/links/56b08c7e08ae9c1968b72026/Blooms-Taxonomy.pdf.

begin the process of self-analyzing, understanding, and accepting your past experiences and your present situation by applying critical thinking.

Most important of all, you will remember, in complete awe, who you used to be. You will suddenly remember what your dreams used to be, and you will begin to acknowledge, perhaps for the first time, how the moment you were violated, both physically and spiritually, your perceptions of yourself and others suddenly shifted and left you on a deserted island, with survival as the only option.

Moreover, you will understand that you were at one point a victim, as described in my find-the-way steps. This process of self-discovery, as I like to call it, will guide you into the habit of *asking*. However, asking what? Asking the ultimate question: "How will this research or inquiry assist me in becoming the person I want and know I can become?"

What are your thoughts, and how have they helped or not helped you in your daily life? Where are you at this point? What have you done up to now? The outcome of Bloom's taxonomy takes you to *create*, which takes you right back to your goal: becoming the "thriving" you. When we are thriving, we are in creation mode, and we start to understand that there are really no limits, nor have there ever been any limits, but the ones imposed on us by our understanding of the good and bad experiences we have faced. It is then when we realize that the creation of a better life for us is possible.

This self-help guide dares you to look beyond your circumstances to merge into becoming the perfect creation, described by you. It dares you to break that boundary between you and those you identify as successful or fulfilled. It will help you acknowledge that you *are* worthy and capable of being that person. At your fingertips, you have all the resources to be successful. In your continuous asking, you will start to understand that you are the only true resource you need to start your journey to become who you have always envisioned yourself to be. As James Allen expressed in his talked-about essay titled "As a Man Thinketh":

> Man can only thus become by discovering within himself the laws of thought, which discovery is totally a matter of application, self-analysis, and experience. ...

48

Thought in the mind hath made us. What we are by thought we wrought and built.[19]

At this point, you should be exhilarated to know that as you start to ask it all, you are just touching the surface in your journey to reconnect with the true self-confident, fearless, and loving *you*. Start asking about and questioning everything. Analyze how others who have gone through dilemmas like being sexually abused have transitioned and become thriving individuals. Ask how they were able to build the courage to move beyond their own overwhelming and even demoralizing and depressing circumstances. How did they move beyond abuse, poverty, discrimination, racism, deceit, violence, etc.?

I cannot emphasize enough the need for you to *ask*. Asking will help you break those imaginary limits you have created between you and those who have or are accomplishing the things you would like to accomplish as well. Let go of the unnecessary excuses that have kept you from moving forward.

Let me reiterate: you need to ask, ask, ask! Question *everything*, even if you do not have the answers. In due time, those questions will linger long enough in your mind, until you finally and somehow come to terms with them, reaching self-acceptance. You may discover that without these experiences, self-imposed or not, you would not be the special and unique person you are. You will see how those events have molded you to be who you are at this very moment.

The same thing has happened to many, including Dr. Maya Angelou, Oprah Winfrey, Martin Luther King Jr., Walt Disney, and Billy Hayes. In the following pages, you will see how their own unique good and bad experiences led them to be who they were meant to be. Therefore, it will be to your advantage to question the "Why?" of your actions and behaviors. Ask the "Why?" of your feelings, the "Why?" of your doubts, jealousy, frustrations, sadness, and motivation, to start on

---

[19] . Accessed October 30, 2022, from https://wahiduddin.net/thinketh/as_a_man_thinketh.pdf.https://wahiduddin.net/thinketh/as_a_man_thinketh.pdf.

the path toward eliminating the bridge between who you are and the person you want to be.

Most, if not all, individuals at one point in their life will face a bump in the road, as I like to refer to when we are facing a dilemma or a problem. What's important is to recognize it for what it is, a bump—a small insignificant bump that you must leave behind, but not before dissecting and understanding it in its full facet.

Pick a famous person you look up to. Think of how this individual has been able to be effective in life after a traumatic experience. How do they view life in general? How do they motivate themselves? What made the difference for them? I believe that in general, it is not that they are a genius or have a higher intelligence quotient (IQ). What they do have is the remarkable ability to see past their experiences and recognizing that there was more for them to do and accomplish. They somehow developed the ability to look within and accept who they were and what they had been through, then internalize that they would not let a circumstance determine their fate. They made a decision that nothing would keep them from becoming who they were meant to be. In other words, the event, whatever it was, would not determine who or what they would become. It was an experience that they learned from and accepted with the apparent bad and good.

The individuals who will be described in this chapter will take you on a journey of self-discovery. You will briefly learn about their experiences and how, despite the dilemmas they faced, they managed to move on to becoming the thriving individuals they knew they were meant to be within their society, communities, home, and to the individual that mattered the most: *themselves!* You will find how creating the habit of asking will guide you to learn more about how things are attainable and how you are just as capable as anyone in attaining your dreams.

A short excerpt of "And Still I Rise"[20] by Dr. Maya Angelou:

You may write me down in history,
with your bitter, twisted lies,
You may tread me in the very dirt,
But still, like dust, I'll rise …
Did you want to see me broken?
Bowed head and lowered eyes?
Shoulders falling like teardrops.
Weakened by soulful cries …
You may shoot me with your words,
You may cut me with your eyes,
You may kill me with your hatefulness,
But still, like air, I'll rise …

DR. MAYA ANGELOU'S STORY

Dr. Maya Angelou was a great author of many wonderful books, including her autobiography, *I Know Why the Caged Bird Sings*.[21] The poetic and powerful words she wrote in this autobiography moved many, making it a top seller in an era where the topic of being sexually abused was more of a taboo than it is nowadays. She not only authored many books, but she was also a well-known poet, playwright, stage and screen performer, and director. As successful as she was, it may come as a shock that she was struck with turmoil beginning early in her childhood.

Not only was Dr. Maya Angelou born in a period where the color of your skin was a big factor for discrimination, she was also abandoned by her parents and sent to live with her paternal grandmother in her

[20] . Maya Angelou, "And Still I Rise: A Books of Poems," copyright ©1978, https://www.hollandcsd.org/cms/lib/NY19000531/Centricity/Domain/74/Still%20I%20Rise%20pdf.pdf.
[21] . Maya Angelou, "I Know Why the Caged Bird Sings," Bantam Books published by arrangement with Random House, Inc., Bantam edition 1971.

early years. Then, at the age of eight years old, she was taken from her grandmother to live again with her mother. While living with her mother, she was raped by the man who was her mother's boyfriend at the time.

Angelou was found by her mother and younger brother Bailey and was taken to the hospital, where she spoke out about her abuse to her family. Months later, she found out about her perpetrator's death, which threw her into a state of guilt and shock. She thought she had caused his death. This shock caused her to fall into a state of selective mutism that lasted approximately five years. During that time, she resorted to books and read, read, read. I believe that, during this time, she was unconsciously transitioning into the Dr. Maya Angelou she is known as today.

Can you believe Dr. Maya Angelou felt she caused the death of her rapist because she spoke out about being sexually abused? She was not aware that *she* was the victim, and that for victims, a normal tendency is to feel guilt and shame. Her lack of knowing and poor thought pattern caused her to live in silence.

How did she bring down that wall of guilt and shame and begin to strive? Do you think this traumatic experience hindered her from becoming the thriving individual she is known for today? Dr. Maya Angelou refused to let her trials and tribulations keep her from getting the best of her life. Her example of courage and being able to find her true essence will live on forever. Angelou subconsciously had the longing for something better, and this allowed her to find the courage necessary to improve upon herself to eventually thrive.

Dr. Maya Angelou always emphasized courage as the most important of all virtues,[22] and it is imperative that you have the necessary courage to start working on yourself via the mode of *asking, asking, asking*. Asking what? Asking how individuals who have faced incredible personal hardship still manage to move beyond their circumstances to fulfill their own dreams. What were their thinking patterns? Then reflect on your experience and ask yourself:

---

[22] . CNN, "Anderson Cooper and Maya Angelou UNCUT interview 08/28/2013 PART 2," YouTube, https://www.youtube.com/watch?v=W3eWGQdho5g

- Who am I?
- What are my own perceptions or irrational thoughts?
- Where do I stand today?
- Am I in real control of who I am?
- Am I happy?
- Am I ready to courageously continue my path toward finding the best of me?

ON SELF-CONDEMNATION

What most commonly shadows victims of sexual abuse is self-condemnation. The victims are, without realizing it, trapped in a repeated cycle of blaming themselves, with overwhelming feelings of guilt and shame. This cycle of self-condemnation can drain all your energy, and a fraction of this feeling can be like what comes when you encounter a lamentable situation, such as having to be tied down to a job with a lousy boss who exploits you and puts you down, demeaning you, creating feelings of shame and unworthiness.

In self-condemnation, you are the lousy boss. In your mind, you are the one who is constantly demeaning and devaluing your worth. In other words, it is your thoughts that are continuously building or destroying the essence of you and keep you from reaching self-actualization as described by American psychologist Abraham Maslow in his hierarchy of needs.[23] Inadvertently, you are the main protagonist responsible for creating a vicious cycle that involves ongoing feelings of shame and guilt.

As your own boss, you should be the one in control of managing those emotions and thoughts, instead of letting your emotions or thoughts overpower you. Keep asking, are you your own boss? Are you ready to steer yourself toward a more fulfilling and happier mindset? Asking who you are will lead you in the direction of accepting, working, learning, and breaking out of the mindset of self-condemnation. During

---

[23] . Joaquin Selva, "What Is Self-Actualization? Meaning, Theory + Examples," *Positive Psychology*, revised April 26, 2023, https://positivepsychology.com/self-actualization/.

this process, the most fundamental ingredient is to have the courage to break barriers to be able to move forward.

Practicing this simple act of asking will assist you in realizing that you are also capable of thriving. Now ask yourself: *If Dr. Maya Angelou was able to thrive after this, why can't I?* Why can't you?

When you ask, you ponder and discover that individuals who have experienced unfortunate challenges have managed to thrive. How did this happen? Can you find a pattern? If you look closely, aside from their conscious or unconscious decision to manage their own thoughts and be their own boss, it is a pattern of having confidence, perseverance, determination, and dedication that has helped individuals thrive, and not a product that relied on luck.

Julian B. Rotter, known for developing influential theories such as the social learning theory, believed "that personality represents an interaction of the individual with his or her environment."[24] He introduced the generalized concept of *locus of control,* which determines how people get reinforced, indicating that much of our personal outcome in life is a result of our attitude or self-determination. He suggests that commonly, individuals may fall under the internal or external locus of control spectrum, being classified along a continuum between extremely internal to extremely external.[25]

As you read, evaluate what you have a tendency to lean toward. Be alert as to where in the locus of control spectrum you fall the most. Identifying where you are in the spectrum within the external and internal locus of control is extremely important in your pursuit of thriving.

Internal Locus of Control

According to Rotter, those with internal locus of control have the following characteristics:

- more often take responsibility for their actions

[24] . Jack Mearns, "The Social Learning Theory of Julian B. Rotter (1916-2014)," accessed October 30, 2022, http://psych.fullerton.edu/jmearns/rotter.htm.
[25] . Mearns, "The Social Learning Theory of Julian B. Rotter (1916-2014)."

- are less influenced by the opinions of others
- most often have a strong sense of being in control of their behavior and environment and motivation
- work harder to achieve and prepare for the things they want
- feel more confident when facing challenges
- are more independent
- generally admit to being happier

In other words, people with a strong sense of self are more responsible for their life and its outcome, and believe that success or failure is due to their own efforts.[26]

External Locus of Control

As per Rotter and in retrospect, individuals with external locus of control believe that the reinforcers in life are controlled by luck. People with high external locus of control tend to blame outside forces for their situation. Thus, they may lack resilience and the confidence necessary to change their circumstances through their own efforts, and they frequently feel hopeless or powerless when faced with difficult situations or decisions. As a result, as per Rotter, they are increasingly prone to learned helplessness.

Briefly, learned helplessness, according to psychologist Martin Seligman, is "when a person begins to believe that they have no control over a situation, even when they do." The mantra of the person who suffers from learned helplessness presumably, and as per Seligman, is: "What is the point in trying?" I add, "Why try? I will probably fail again." Meanwhile, an individual with a high internal locus of control's likely reaction would be, "I did not do so well, but I will try harder … I can do this!" Ultimately, thinking optimistically is a key predictor of how you will find your way to be the thriving individual you are meant to be.[27]

[26] . Kendra Cherry, "Locus of Control and Your Life," Verywell Mind, accessed October 17, 2022, https://www.verywellmind.com/what-is-locus-of-control-2795434.
[27] . "Learned Helplessness," Out of the Fog, https://outofthefog.website/what-not-to-do-1/2015/12/3/learned-helplessness.

OPRAH WINFREY'S STORY

When people hold on to the toughest moments of their past, they're short-changing their futures.—Bishop T.D. Jakes, during Oprah Winfrey Life class, 2013

When discussing an individual like Oprah Winfrey, we would say that she is an example of an individual with a strong internal locus of control, and one who has chosen not to shortchange her future regardless of her circumstance. One would think she was born on a bed of gold. However, this inspiring African American, thriving media proprietor, actress, producer, philanthropist, and multi-award-winning talk-show hostess—who, according to *Forbes*, is currently worth 3 billion dollars[28], was not born with all the conditions to meet success.

Considering Oprah Winfrey and her present situation, it is hard to imagine someone like her experiencing sexual abuse or anything traumatic. However, from a young age, Oprah faced many trials and tribulations. At the tender age of nine, Oprah was raped by a cousin and then was a repeat victim of sexual abuse by kin.[29] I remind you that with such abuse may come the long-term effects discussed in chapter 3, such as ripples of confusion, guilt, and shame that may last a lifetime. I may sound presumptuous saying such a thing, but Oprah's success proves that she was able to confront and move past the effects that might have permanently hindered her.

Aside from being sexually abused, Oprah also confronted the covert and overt effects of living in an era of blunt gender and racial discrimination while living in chronic poverty, where potato sacks were

---

[28] . Kathleen Elkins, "From Poverty to a $3 Million Fortune—The Incredible Rags-to-Riches Story of Oprah Winfrey," *Business Insider* (May 28, 2015), https://www.businessinsider.com/rags-to-riches-story-of-oprah-winfrey-2015-5#:~:text=As%20a%20child%2C%20Oprah%20Winfrey%20wore%20potato%20sacks,list%20of%20the%20400%20richest%20people%20in%20America.

[29] . "Young Oprah Winfrey Interview on Her Life and Career (1991)," *Manufacturing Intellect* (August 26, 2017), YouTube, https://www.youtube.com/watch?v=1ObDKKW-sn8.

a common wardrobe even for her. The odds seemed to always be against her, but again, time proved her to have enough belief in herself and courage to face all these hardships. Going back to having a strong internal locus of control, I believe that for Oprah, this was a key factor in moving past her circumstances, one step at a time.

Oprah's unquestionable bravery enabled her to *advance on the Chaos and the Dark* to eventually thrive. Her courage and determination to thrive from her experience has paved the way to bring more awareness to our society about child sexual abuse. With the help of many, she has worked diligently to bring awareness and prevention to the crippling effects of child sexual abuse. This is apparent in her work to help create the National Child Protection Act, informally known as the Oprah Bill, signed and approved by President Bill Clinton in 1993.

In 1991, her testimony to the Senate in favor of the National Child Protection Act helped to ensure its passage. The Oprah Bill gives the population the right to have laws protecting youth from criminals. The bill creates awareness by allowing the public to have access to the files of such offenders. The name of any criminal involved in child abuse, sex offenses, violent crime, arson, or felony drug charges can now be publicly accessed through an internet database, thanks to Oprah's contribution in making this possible.[30]

Even today, Oprah continues to contribute much in her constant attempt to raise awareness of child sexual abuse and the many other social problems we face. What is even more moving is that she has tried to remain humble and give some of her knowledge back to us. If you pay close attention to Oprah, you will observe that she is just a person like you and me. Nonetheless, there is something that has and continues to set her apart, and that is her courage, which many lack but that can be built upon. Her willingness to be courageous and intuitively know that there is much more to life than merely surviving is evident. Her actions and success make it obvious to me that at one point in her life, she was courageous enough to look herself in the mirror and accept and admit

[30] . "Child Protection Act Signing, C-SPAN.org, video, accessed October 30, 2022, https://www.c-span.org/video/?53236-1/child-protection-act-signing.

that internally, there was much work needed to become the person she envisioned herself to be. When people are truly being themselves and are conscious of who they are and what they want, nothing and no one can keep them from becoming who they are meant to be.

Looking yourself in the mirror and coming to terms with who you are can set the stage for positive change—a change that will give you a taste of what freedom to be yourself is all about. Again, it will take an enormous amount of courage to accept and face your traumatic experience, especially to reflect and say, "This is not working for me," and then be able to ask "Why?" This awareness will eventually daunt you that *you* are the individual ultimately responsible for what your life currently is and will be.

However, remember that Oprah's success did not come about without a good attitude, much preparation, and vigorous effort when she was faced with challenges along her way (which are all indicators of having a strong internal locus of control). *You* are the catalyst for change, not an external force. Only *you* and believing in yourself can make the difference. Oprah's life is proof that believing in yourself and having the courage to continue despite the odds makes a world of a difference. In my opinion, this is the exact message she has tried to convey to her audience for decades: that if you really believe in yourself, anything is possible.

If you have not done so already, you will be astounded to learn that there is so much to accomplish and change based on your current situation. Therefore, I urge you to put your "curiosity bug" in operation and ask yourself these questions:

- Do I want to remain stagnant, frozen in time, because of what someone attempted to make my fate?
- Will I be the one in control of my own fate and keep working toward finding the best of me?
- Will I continue to shortchange my future because of others' past failure to respect my basic rights as a person?
- Will I continue to focus on and give power to those who violated me?

• Will I start being there for me, for a change?

Being a person with a strong internal locus of control can bring you many benefits, rather than merely relying on external forces for your advancement. Knowing what courage truly entails will bring positive change. Then and only then will positive change become the norm in your life.

Therefore, I want to continue to emphasize the importance of having courage, which is needed to look within to acknowledge that there are many irrational thoughts to work on. Irrational thoughts can be described as having erroneous and even exaggerated perceptions of yourself and your relationships with others. Courage is needed to move on to "trust yourself, your intuition, and your nature," as the transcendentalist poet and philosopher Ralph Waldo Emmerson emphasized in his acclaimed essay, "Self-Reliance":

> We are now men and must accept in the highest mind the same transcendent destiny; and not minors and invalids in a protected corner, not cowards fleeing before a revolution, but guides, redeemers, and benefactors, obeying the Almighty effort, and advancing on Chaos and the Dark.[31]

These powerful words describe an individual facing hardship while making the decision to confront or avoid the situation (fight or flight). In essence, if you choose to confront the hardship, there are many life-changing benefits that will certainly transform you into becoming a person of substance. You become that guide, redeemer, benefactor; you become a better you.

Imagine having a healthier mindset in which guilt and shame are no longer the driving force behind your actions. Imagine the goals and dreams you are capable of accomplishing. You have the tools necessary to start becoming the person you are meant to become. The individuals mentioned above prove it can be done, if you believe in yourself and

---

[31] . http://www.emersoncentral.com/selfreliance.htm.

have enough faith and courage to persevere despite the odds. You are not alone; you have them, and you have me, Lola Lola. You have this self-help-guide and many others working on helping to improve this world to make it a better place. But it all starts with *you*.

Feeling alone is not an option; you have a million others nationwide who have experienced a similar story to yours or worse. There are others, a few of whom will be briefly discussed, who although they were not necessarily sexually abused, had to overcome other types of trauma.

DR. MARTIN LUTHER KING'S STORY

When you think of Dr. Martin Luther King Jr., your immediate thought may be that he was a legendary civil rights activist. Perhaps you also visualize him standing at the podium on August 28, 1963, when he suddenly changed the script and started his legendary "I Have a Dream" speech, where he shared his dream of equal rights for all. We may see him as a person who persevered in his fight for freedom, justice, and equality for all, and it may be normal to envision him as having been born this flawless creation of a man. Considering the significance he has had in history, you can even think he was a genius of justice with the utmost compassion.

There is no doubt he will always serve as an important figure to our society. However; one of the biggest ideas we create is the notion that people such as MLK are superhuman and that there is no way we can compare ourselves to them. In reality, if you do your own asking, you will learn that he was a person just like you and me. Therefore, it is of urgency that we break down the wall that many tend to create that separates us from Martin Luther King Jr. or any other person of substance who has made such contributions to society. As an individual, you *can* accomplish things important or transcendent as he did if you just believe in yourself.

If you are curious enough to *ask*, you may become aware that you have an inaccurate perception of those who have managed to thrive in their lifetime. When you do your own investigation and really magnify a person's life, you will find that often, there are hardships to overcome and sometimes unimaginable and devastating trauma. Dr. Martin Luther King Jr. did face trauma and hardship. He was the voice for many in a time where it was possible for colored men to be killed for just speaking up for their own rights, let alone representing the rights of other colored men and women.

Dr. Martin Luther King Jr. faced threats not just against himself but toward his family, which more than likely put him in a state of anguish and doubt as to whether he should continue his fight for equal rights. Did he have doubts at one point in time? I would say yes, wouldn't you? It is without discussion that he faced much hardship and struggle, especially when all he did was speak out consistently about the need for equal rights without engaging in violence at a time when violence was the norm against blacks who would speak out.[32]

Before a person can be described as *thriving* and fight for a cause that has such deep meaning, there must be a realization that positive results come hand in hand with human struggle, sacrifice, and perhaps even grief. Dr. Martin Luther King Jr. faced the problem of injustice, as many of us have, but instead of hiding behind his shadow, he had the courage to stay focused on what he believed in and to fight for equality for all, no matter the outcome. He never stopped believing it was possible.

Facing his fears did unfortunately take his life but proved once again the importance of living according to your rules, your beliefs, your passion, and your love. As long as we have respect for others, this is something we are all capable of doing. As long as you believe it is possible and find the courage to face the hidden fear of being you, you can find your way to living a life that is meaningful to you and perhaps to many others.

It is imperative to focus on your ongoing accomplishments—the little steps that will eventually lead to where you want to be. Dr. Martin Luther King's goal was to have equal rights for all, and thanks to his courage in the face of fear, he was able to talk about his dreams,

---

[32] . "Martin Luther King Jr.: Biographical," The Nobel Prize, https://www.nobelprize. org/prizes/peace/1964/king/biographical/.

paving the way for many to continue the fight for civil rights. Dr. Maya Angelou, who we discussed earlier, also met, worked with, and became friends with Dr. Martin Luther King Jr. during their fight for civil rights. She says that "we need people with courage and understood courage as being one of the most important virtues as without courage you can't practice any other virtue consistently."[33]

When reading and learning about individuals like Dr. Martin Luther King Jr., you discover a tremendous amount of courage to face fear and obstacles along the way and to still manage to voice and be who they are despite anyone's opinion or belief of them. This takes you back to your need to level yourself with these thriving individuals and internalize the truth that you are just like them—an individual with dreams, an individual with a purpose, with the need to make a significant difference not just in the life of others but, exclusively important, in your own.

You as an individual have the capacity to make your dreams come true and to become the thriving individual you are meant to be. Nevertheless, you must practice being courageous. Courageous to be you, to first look within and figure out *you,* to then begin the process slowly toward becoming the thriving individual you see yourself to be.

While questioning or *asking,* be attentive to the metamorphosis that the individual endured and the connecting steps that lead him or her to become that thriving individual. This focus will allow you to pay closer attention to your own metamorphosis and how you will become an active and conscious actor in your continuous transformation to be that individual you envision. This will allow you to break the barriers you have unconsciously built, rationalizing that we are all more alike than different. Understand that your dreams are also attainable, just like Martin Luther King Jr's dreams or Oprah's, with the potential to transcend to unimagined heights, in spite of the odds.

---

[33] . Anderson Cooper and Maya Angelou, personal communication, CNN, August 28, 2013.

WALT DISNEY'S STORY

This takes us to my next and favorite question: Can you imagine a world without Disney World? Who was Walt Disney? Have you ever wondered how his success came about? What and how many obstacles did he face before attaining his success? How was he able to overcome his difficulties, to be able to gain the empire he left behind? Unbelievably, Walt Disney too struggled in many ways and dealt with many setbacks before becoming the successful icon we know of today.

At a tender age, he gained a love for animation, and he opened his own film studio, Laugh-O-Gram, by the age of twenty. Unfortunately, this did not last; the film studio went downhill, and with forty dollars in his pocket, he moved to a new city in pursuit of opportunities. Once there, he started the Disney Brothers Studio with his brother, Roy, and created a few of his successful animation characters: Oswald the Lucky Rabbit and the Alicia Cartoons. Disappointingly, a New York distributor he worked for stripped Walt Disney of his prestigious animation characters and stole the rights for those creations, along with the animators he thought were on his "team."

Do you think that after being violated and having to start over for the third time, Disney would stop pursuing his dream? No. Walt Disney continued to believe in himself enough to keep working on his dream. With his brother, his wife, and his loyal friend Iwerk, Walt went on to produce brilliant cartoons featuring his epic animated character, Mickey Mouse.

As you may have noticed, Disney's success did not happen overnight. If he would have allowed the situations he faced to get the best of him, such as the losing of his first business or the disloyalty of individuals he trusted, it could have been the end of his career.[34]

Walt was a person just like you, yet he had dreams and enough self-confidence and courage to not let his negative experiences get the best of him. Was it easy? Absolutely not! He had to continue believing, just as you must. I believe that somehow, he knew that the actions of others

---

[34] . "Walt Disney," Biography.com (2014).

had nothing to do with *him*. He accepted this, understood it, and had enough courage to continue working toward the things he wanted to accomplish.

Did he face doubt? Did he face sadness? Did he face confusion? Did he face fear in the face? Of course, but Walt had enough courage to continue believing in the most important person: himself. He believed he was capable of making his dreams come true, and he did.

If he did it, you can too. Instead of coming up with excuses for what you cannot do because of the drawbacks, problems, or experiences life throws at you, you may want to *ask* yourself, *How will I beat this stumbling block that is keeping me from making progress towards what I want to accomplish? How can I learn from this unwanted experience to make sure it does not happen again? How can I stick to trusting that I am the main component to my success?*

BILLY HAYES'S STORY

For me, the word *curiosity* opens doors for growth, making all things approachable. It allows a person to understand that no being or circumstance is inaccessible and that we are all capable of making our dreams come true regardless of the situation. And as Billy Hayes expressed, "Never give up, no matter how deep you are, you can find your way out, there is a way out, just stay at it."[35]

Hayes relates his own self-imposed experience in a Turkish prison, where he justly served his four-year mandatory sentence. However, Billy Hayes was to be made an example of, and after his four-year sentence, he was unlawfully sentenced to another thirty years in prison. He had been sentenced for smuggling marijuana, which, as he has expressed in many interviews, was not such a clever idea. He further explains that he found himself in the darkest of days and confirms that from this self-imposed negativity in which he managed to place himself, he was

---

[35] . Billy Hayes interview, "Riding the Midnight Express" (November 6, 2014), YouTube, broadway.com. https://www.youtube.com/watch?v=ZN6WZr_Wz_4.

able to find peace within. He emphasizes that no matter what you are going through or what situation you are in, there is always a way out.

Within the walls of the Turkish prison, "midnight express" was a phrase used to talk about escape. It later became the title of Hayes's successful book, which eventually became an Academy Award–winning movie. The years he spent paying for his mistakes set the stage for his welcome transition to becoming the thriving individual he was meant to be. Within those prison walls, Billy found *Billy*. He ironically found freedom.

Billy was able to look within and deal with his own demons of fear and irrational beliefs, finally learning the ultimate lesson: love of self and love to all. Billy's experience again emphasizes that only when we have the courage to look within to confront and accept our feelings of shame, fear, and doubt, and our self-imposed traumas or the ones innocently placed upon us, can we find our true essence, our calling, the true thriving individual inside of each of us so many times emphasized in this guide. Knowing who you are liberates you from your own judgment and criticism, as you realize that at the end of it all, we are all connected to one another, and we are all here to learn from our experiences. Moving on from shame, guilt, sadness, and disgust is possible.

Billy opens our mind and attempts to convey that out of a terrible experience, whether you contributed to it or not, can come freedom of self and the courage you need to become the person you envision yourself to be. He puts great emphasis on the importance of not giving up at any point in your life. As he put it, "If you manage to stay at it, you will find the inner freedom and success you search for."[36]

Looking within your own self-imposed victim walls, you can find freedom. Fear, panic, shame, and irrational thoughts or perceptions are usually the aftermath of a traumatic experience that can be dissipated or transformed into the best learning experience of your life. Only after you cleanse your mind, body, and soul from these feelings will you be able to

---

[36] . "Midnight Express truth revealed by Alinur Part-1," TDTKB, YouTube, https://youtu.be/pHjLMnGkedU.

experience the true meaning of freedom.[37] Billy Hayes's experience was meaningful and with a depth that can hardly be explained in words, although his attempt via his book, interviews, film, etc., was truly a magnificent one.

I believe what made this a great example to add here is that Billy explains, maybe not in these same words, how he was almost broken but somehow something ignited in him that kept him from giving in to his immediate environment, thus allowing him to not give up on his hope to someday be on the other side of those prison walls. Billy not only managed to escape prison but also to escape the prison within. He was able to accept his experience and bring consolation through the sharing of his story. He accepted himself completely, and in the process was able to thrive. At times, escaping actual prison walls can be easier than escaping the prison walls built within. Hence the power of his shared story.

Billy Hayes was obviously not a perfect person, making a few too many bad choices, including smuggling marijuana into another country. However, in his darkest days, he chose life. He chose life by recognizing his part in the present situation, accepting it, and having the courage to look within to find answers. In a nutshell, he made the best of his situation. He confronted it head-on with courage, love, and compassion for the person who needed it most: himself.

You know how hard it is to deal with a situation when you feel victimized but attempt to imagine how hard it is to admit to your own failures and shortcomings. It is usually easier to point the finger and say, "Because of you, I am this way." Pointing the finger at yourself and saying, "I am in this situation because of the decisions I made" can take a toll, and you may need to triple the courage attribute.

Imagine how hard it is to search within after confronting a traumatic experience that you know you brought on yourself, contributing to an undesirable consequence for you and your loved ones. That's why *asking* is so important, as knowing about how others turned their own self-defeating behaviors into a total act of courage and a finding of self,

---

[37] . Billy Hayes revisits *Midnight Express* interview.

changing their possible negative outcome into a personal triumph, can serve as the needed inspiration for you to be effective in your own life.

Many of us have support from others yet think we are alone, desperately and maybe even unconsciously searching for that helping hand or that superman or superwoman who will come in and rescue us from ourselves or from our sad fate. However, if you look closely, *asking* will help you become aware that the superman or superwoman is and has always been within you. The superman and the superwoman have been in your footsteps all this time. The superman and the superwoman in you has been exposed, and now you must make use of them—or better yet, yourself.

In his journey to become the person he was meant to be, Billy repeatedly teaches us about the importance of taking responsibility for all our good or bad actions and to understand that they have consequences. In other words, when you are faced with any kind of situation, no matter how big or small your part is, you always have a part in it, and your part will determine the positive or negative consequences that come out of that situation.

Keep asking yourself: *Why didn't they give up?* They continued, despite their own trials and tribulations, so why can't you? You are not hugely different from Dr. Maya Angelou, Oprah Winfrey, Dr. Martin Luther King Jr., Walt Disney, or Billy Hayes. Whether your problems are self-imposed or not, you can be just as successful when overcoming the many barriers that life throws at you, just as they did. You too can keep on going!

Keep in mind that, as I have mentioned repeatedly in this guide, there is one major difference between the individuals previously mentioned and you. They worked on being courageous every step of the way. Their first courageous act was to look within, to challenge their thoughts, their irrational beliefs, their perceptions of others, their own upbringing, and their present circumstances.

Knowing and courageously accepting who you are and being comfortable in your own skin will set the stage for change at any level. You will know who you are. You will grow stronger and be able to face many challenges. This is a gift that will last a lifetime. All the individuals mentioned above faced many trials, yet they had the audacity and courage to continue to persevere.

Look closer and see where their courage to continue despite their odds led them. Dr. Maya Angelou with her teachings and poems has helped many. Walt Disney created Disneyland and Disney World, where many children and adults enjoy themselves. Even to this day, we believe in the idea, and whether overtly or covertly work toward Martin Luther King's Jr. dream of "freedom for all."

Can you imagine for one second what would have happened if they had given up when faced with a challenge in life? Can you imagine not celebrating Martin Luther King Jr. Day? Can you imagine not having the privilege of reading Dr. Maya Angelou's autobiography, *I Know Why the Caged Bird Sings*, and one of her most successful poems, "Phenomenal Woman"? Can you imagine life without Disney World or Mickey and Minnie? This shows us repeatedly how one person can have an influence on not just their own world but that of others. It shows that if you finally have the courage to take over the superman or superwoman role that has been yours all along, you can make a significant difference in your life.

It is not by chance, and these individuals are not different from you or I. They are just people who developed an abundance of courage that allowed them to continue amidst their trials and tribulations in life. Do not doubt that there is success waiting for you if you courageously continue to challenge yourself. *Ask*: what is my term of identification? What step am I in? Am I the victim? The survivor? The accomplisher? The striver? The thriving individual? Where are you taking your recent discovery of self-identification in this guide?

One thing to keep in mind is that you do not have to accomplish the same as the individuals mentioned above. Everyone starts and ends differently, and you are not them. *It is even better: you are you!* You are a wonderful person with different dreams, stories, and unique talents that everyone around will just love to know about, even you. You *do* want to make all efforts in reaching the final step of the "thriving you" to make your dreams come true and find your true purpose in life.

Everyone's purpose is different. Maybe your purpose is to become a thriving business owner of a bar by the age of fifty. If so, research Jon Taffer from Bar Rescue, and you will be in for a big surprise to learn about the people who inspire him the most and how stepping outside the box or the bubble is possible. Maybe you see yourself working with the developmentally disabled using dolphin–human therapy. Can you picture yourself in the Keys swimming with the dolphins? I know I can! Whatever your purpose is, it can be done.

Moreover, know you are not the only, nor are you the first person in the world who will have to face personal challenges before becoming the *thriving* individual you intend to become. Understand that it will be a long ride with many little insignificant bumps before you get to where you want to be. However, be conscious that it will be the best ride you will ever be on. There is not and will never be any ride at Disney World or any other place better than this ride, to that I can attest.

This ride will free you of many inhibitions, irrational thoughts, false beliefs, unnecessary guilt, unnecessary shame, and on and on. This ride will free you from *you*. This possibility needs to be tightly ingrained within your mind and soul. Believe it is possible and have the courage to keep on going despite the odds, the hurts, and the let-downs—despite you and your own self-imposed limitations.

Lola Lola dares you to have enough courage to wake up daily to work on you, as there is nothing greater than *self*. As actor Jim Carrey, from movies like *The Mask* and *Ace Ventura Pet Detective* to name a few, said in a speech, "Risk being seen in all your glory."[38]

All these thriving individuals mentioned, passed or not, repeatedly faced fear, self-doubt, deception, mistakes, pain, and struggle in the face, to eventually show us that becoming the thriving individual you envision yourself to be is possible. However, becoming that which you want to become will not happen if you do not have the courage to stand up for yourself first.

Learning about how different individuals have had to face challenging traumas in their life will help you remember, especially on

---

[38] . Jim Carrey, "This Is How to Be Bigger Than Yourself," Goalcast (May 6, 2016), YouTube, https://youtu.be/IHHF8h-zcas.

those days that your courage and strength are at their weakest, that you are not alone and are moving past this and thriving. *Asking* will serve as a motivator to get you back on track in your journey to pursue your own dreams.

In my opinion, a man without dreams is a walking dead man. We each have our calling and our own struggles. What we sometimes lack is faith in ourselves and a whole lot of courage. It *will* take tremendous courage, arduous work, faith, confidence, and unconditional love toward the person who will need it the most: yourself.

CHAPTER 5

YOU ARE NOT ALONE: STATISTICS

D o you know that, unfortunately, you are not alone? Are you truly conscious of how often children are being sexually abused? As a nation and a community, do you think we can afford to continue turning a blind eye to the magnitude of the problem of sexual abuse of children? Do you think it is fair to you that you prolong your healing process anymore?

The following statistics will demonstrate the urgent need for this self-help guide—and the need for individuals to have the courage to become empowered after having been exposed to such horrific and demoralizing abuse. Via your self-empowerment, our work to end this crime against innocent children, which has been going on for centuries, will begin to make a difference.

SEXUAL ABUSE STATISTICS

These statistics are taken from Lauren's Kids: Sexual Abuse Mission Organization:[39]

- "There are 42 million childhood sexual survivors in the U.S." *How does this make you feel?*

---

[39] . Lauren's Kids, "A guide to hope & healing: National Statistics, 2021," https://www.youtube.com/watch?v=ZN6WZr_Wz_4. https://laurenskids.org/awareness/about-faqs/facts-and-stats/

- "Approximately 20% of sexual abuse victims are younger than 8." *Younger than 8—this could be your niece or nephew, your child, or your grandchild. During your own self-analysis, ask, "Can we continue being quiet about our own abuse when perhaps we can prevent it from happening to others in the long run?*

- "90% of sexual abuse victims know the perpetrator in some way." *Are we paying close attention to our immediate surroundings and the behaviors of those we love? Are we really observing those close to our children, even though they may be familiar friends/family we love and treasure?*

- "*1 in 3* girls and *1 in 5* boys are sexually abused before the age of 18." *How many alarming statistics do we need before we do something as a community or as a nation? How much longer will you remain in the common hideouts that deter your thriving path?*

- "1 in 5 children is solicited sexually while on the internet before the age of 18." *Are we keeping an eye on our children and their interactions on Facebook, Snapchat, Instagram, and so forth? Are we taking the time to educate our children about what is going on out there, and are we providing the necessary tools for them to protect themselves?*

- "30% of child sexual abuse is never reported." *So know that these statistics are an under-representation of child sexual abuse.*

- "70% of all reported sexual assaults (including assaults on adults) occur to children aged 17 and under."

- "95% of sexual abuse can be preventable through education."

- "38% of boys are sexually abused by a female."

- "There is worse lasting emotional damage when a child's sexual abuse started before age of six and lasted for several years. Among child and teen victims of sexual abuse there is a 42% increased chance of suicidal thoughts during adolescents."

Children with developmental disabilities are not free from becoming victims of child sexual abuse. Surprisingly, statistics reveal that they are at a higher risk due to their dependence on caregivers, which includes friends or family members; their tendency for isolation; and their obvious powerlessness due to physical, speech, and communication barriers. In addition, their impaired/limited cognitive abilities, lack of information about abuse and how to prevent it, and unprotected organizational structures and policies also place them at increased risk for any type of abuse, including sexual abuse.[40] Overall, children who are diagnosed with any particular type of disability have a 3.44 higher chance of becoming a victim of some type of abuse when compared to children without disabilities.[41] Furthermore, statistics show that yearly, 325,000 children are at risk of becoming victims of commercial child sexual exploitation.[42]

Abuse of children happens at any socioeconomic status, to both boys and girls, including the ones exposed to social media and in the entertainment industry—thus the reason I decided to include in this guide just a brief list of those in the entertainment industry who have publicly come out and informed the public about their own history with rape and child sexual abuse. I find these individuals to be true heroes, and I respect and admire them deeply for their courage to share with us a glimpse of their history with sexual abuse and willingness to not just survive but thrive. This should inspire and make you even more aware that "you are never alone." Some have even started or participated in the Me Too movement founded by Tarana Burke, which continues to thrive.

Famous Sexual Abuse Victims

1. Tyler Perry (https://www.youtube.com/watch?v=r4saxuqYENs)
2. Carlos Santana (https://www.youtube.com/watch?v=q3U54 KNLoUA)

---

[40] . Leigh Ann Davis M.S.S.W, M.P.A, The Arc, "Abuse of Children with intellectual Disabilities," last revised March 1, 2011, https://thearc.org/wp-content/uploads/forchapters/Child%20Abuse.pdf#:~:text=Children%20with%20any%20type%20of%20disability%20are%203.44,to%20children%20without%20disabilities.%20%28Sullivan%20%26%20Knutson%2C%202000%29.
[41] . Sullivan and Knutson, 2000; "People First Language," The Arc, www.thearc.org/what-we-do/resources/fact-sheets/abuse.
[42] . "Preventing Sexual Child Abuse as Parents and Caregivers," American SPCC, https://americanspcc.org/sexual-child-abuse/.

3. Ellen DeGeneres (molested by stepfather as a young girl; https://www.youtube.com/watch?v=vFBBNElImEc)

4. Tim Roth (sexually abused by grandfather, who also abused his father: directed a film about it called *The War Zone*; https://www.youtube.com/watch?v=NRNVMXgjad8)

5. Marylyn Van Derbur (former Miss America, sexually abused by father ages five through eighteen; wrote *Miss America by Day: Lessons Learned from Ultimate Betrayals and Unconditional Love*; https://www.youtube.com/watch?v=xECQd6ZrbDk

6. Ashley Judd (https://www.youtube.com/watch?v=u06yuXfCNUQ and https://www.youtube.com/watch?v=_kFzOF_qr4o)

7. Teri Hatcher (https://www.youtube.com/watch?v=DtFjGvVAFRU)

8. Tisha Campbell (https://www.youtube.com/watch?v=dXxdm0yYIuA)

9. Gabrielle Union (https://www.youtube.com/watch?v=F2pGls-SxXU)

10. Lady Gaga (raped at age nineteen, wrote a song "Till it Happens to You"; https://www.youtube.com/watch?v=9Am3YibgfKM)

These are just a few of the celebrities who have been victims of child sexual abuse or rape at a young age and were affected by this terrible experience. Regardless, they shared their stories of abuse, shame, guilt, and sadness. After years of suffering, they had enough courage to break the silence to help and alert the many in social media and the general population (female and male, children and young adults) about child sexual abuse and rape and their "zero tolerance" for it.

Not to sound presumptuous, but I assume that they hope to put a stop to this horrific act toward children, teenagers, and young male and female adults. Your decision to work automatically puts you in charge of your circumstance and unites you to this Me Too movement. This is why you never give up on yourself. You are never alone, even if, at times, it may look that way.

Knowing that, as stated by Lauren's Kids, "there are 42 million childhood sexual abuse survivors in the US"[43] should be motivation enough to bring out the best person there is in you. This statistic alone explains the need for this self-help guide, and the need for you to work on *you*. The devastating long-term effects of child sexual abuse are many, and you owe it to yourself to become a whole person again, capable of understanding that there is hope and you are a special and much-needed individual to you, your community, and the nation.

As reflected in these statistics, and as I would like to continuously emphasize through this reading, *you are not alone.* Many children, right this moment, are experiencing such abuse at the hands of the ones responsible for providing them with love and nurture. Thus, the fact that you are not alone is a sad one, yet a concept that you should fully internalize, to serve as a reminder of how important it is that you start to work on yourself with a sense of urgency and an abundance of courage.

By working on *you*, you will eventually start breaking free from all the negative consequences that experiencing such abuse brought to your life. You will learn to hold hands with your silence, pain, guilt, shame, and inability to trust yourself to master the art of ripping all the immeasurable benefits of coming to terms with this terrible experience you had to endure. Let these statistics set the stage for change. Let them be another driving force behind your need to get where you need to go and become the thriving individual you want to become. Let it be a constant reminder that you are not alone and that many, whether voiced or not, depend on your coming out to a more positive, healthy, stable, and capable human being. Remember: I'm OK, you're OK.

---

[43] . National statistics from Lauren's Kids, tweets from Lauren's Kids, https://laurenskids.org/501c3/.

CHAPTER 6

SILENCE

Prior to starting the healing process and the restructuring of most of your thoughts and life in general, and understanding the potential benefits that can come from your choice of silence, it is imperative to ask yourself, "Have I allowed this experience or traumatic situation to take hold not just of my overall physical and mental well-being but my spiritual well-being as well?" Even in the case of sexual abuse, why should you allow anyone to take from you your true essence, your driving force, and for so long? It is good to keep in mind that they may have tampered with your young body, but your spirit, your force, your will, your true essence—why allow that to go too? Why? Who can possibly be so important that you give *you* up for them or that? That is exactly what they tried to do; why are you going to allow it?

Your driving force or spirit stays, and you build on from that. No excuses! Always keep in mind that you have no right to destroy your own self. This is not an option, nor should it ever be, as you do not give anyone power to take away that light, that force within, called your spirit. No experience, no deception, no trauma, no person, nothing should ever have that much power over you. You as an individual have the right to slow down a bit in the face of despair, yet your spirit, your force within, that is yours and no one else's.

When you are stuck in those days of despair, here is a little reminder of how the word *spirit* is defined in the Britannica Dictionary: "a: the force within a person that is believed to give the body life, energy, and power … b: the inner quality or nature of a person."[44]

As a friend of mine once told me, "You get yourself in that field, and keep taking those weeds out, girl." You never give up! You get up and go! *Wow.* Some wonderful people have been on my train, and may God and the universe bless them.

In her book *I Never Told Anyone*, author Louise Thornton wondered why it is that children who have been molested, sexually abused, or even raped rarely ever tell. She wrote, "They never tell for the same reason that anyone who has been helplessly shamed and humiliated, and who is without protection or validation of personal integrity, prefers silence."[45] On the same note, I say that most of the time, unfortunately, silence is no longer an option but a way of life when you have faced such a trauma. As I read this line, I felt the pain flow through my veins, giving me an uncontrollable need to weep. I felt for the first time the depth of my pain as I was able to see all that was taken from me. Then I understood the inexplicable need for silence.

Silence, unbelievably, for some time, can be a good thing, so don't reprimand yourself for remaining silent. Instead, remain in silence, as it is to your advantage if wisely used. If utilized properly, silence will provide you with many benefits. During your time of silence, one benefit that particularly stands out is the sudden awareness of the new you. The new you will be the start of a new life, as this new you will be increasingly aware of herself and her surroundings, will have clearer view of her self-worth, will set new boundaries, and will rekindle her old and probably put-aside dreams.

Keep in mind that, for the sake of this self-help guide, I refer to silence not just as the act of not talking, as in the example previously provided of Dr. Maya Angelou, who in an unconscious attempt to make some sense of her situation desperately resorted to complete muteness

---

[44] . "Spirit," The Britannica Dictionary, https://www.britannica.com/dictionary/spirit.

[45] . Ellen Bass, Louis Thorton, 1991, "I Never Told Anyone: writings by women survivors of child sexual abuse" page 13. First Harper Perennial edition published 1991.

at the age of eight. You can be the greatest public speaker and yet be in complete silence—the silence of your true being, not allowing your true essence to be known, in which your own experiences, doubts, and insecurities are off limits even to those close to you and sometimes even to yourself.

However, let's now consider all that can take place in your time of silence. During your time in silence, you will have time to regroup and get to know yourself. What a wonderful feeling to know who you are. Trust me, it is wonderful! Once you really start knowing who you are, negative experiences, negative people, and bad circumstances turn into opportunities to help you grow as a person instead of putting you down. Silence helps you find peace within. Silence helps you find meaning and teaches you to enjoy your company.

During this time that you have recognized as your time in silence, ask many questions. Ask, "Who knows me? Who truly knows what I am about?" When you have difficulties with others and they have expressed opinions of who you are, have you ever thought to yourself, *Jeez, how wrong they are. They cannot even imagine who I am, where I have been, or where I come from.* If there is much disparity between who you are and what they believe you are, then look within and ask yourself questions. Start by asking, "Who am I? Who is this person that I live with daily?" Yes, you live with yourself, daily? How do you do it? What is your own view of you?

I suggest you learn to indulge in silence. Take this silent time to know about *you*, the core of *you*. Observe your actions, your behavior. Listen to your explanations and your responses to different actions of others. Understand your feelings and the feelings and actions of those around you and learn. Observing your immediate environment in silence and without others knowing is awesome, because you get to see yourself in them and them in you. You start getting a sense of, *Jeez, I may be wrong about a few things* or *Look who my friend is, they have been through x, y, z and have done x, y, z, and look at them, they keep on going, being successful, not letting things bring them down. Maybe I want to be that kind of person—or maybe, just maybe, I can supersede that and go beyond that.*

Indulging in silence can also help you start the process of learning to have patience. All remarkable things, like you, take some time. Have you ever heard the saying "Rome wasn't built in a day?" In the same way, we and the greatness that we can become will not happen in a day.

Silence may give you time to question your circumstances, those around you, yourself, and your world in general. It can be a time to truly see your own tolerance and resilience and build on from where you are. In *Psychology Today*, resilience is defined as "the psychological quality that allows some people to be knocked down by the adversities of life and come back at least as strong as before."[46] Being resilient means learning to use your circumstances to help you come out of a situation triumphant, or simply learn from your experience to then be able to move on to bigger and better things. Silence is just another tool to use to your advantage. It is not a tool for you to dive further into despair but one that, if used effectively and without error, can bring the greatest benefit.

In silence, you can learn to manage your emotions and, as previously stated, improve your ability to exert patience, which is one of the attributes associated with resilience. You build resilience by learning to adapt, learning to accept yourself, learning to understand, and learning to observe yourself and others. You learn to come to terms with yourself, period. You no longer depend on others' reactions for your own reassurance of your worthiness, but you learn of your own worthiness, because you rely on yourself.

Through this time, you are learning to tolerate you. Yes, *you*. Just think: how can you ever truly tolerate others when you cannot tolerate yourself?

What is tolerance? The Cambridge Dictionary defines it as "willingness to accept feelings, habits, or beliefs that are different from your own."[47] It is a willingness to tolerate your own inequities. What? Do you have inequities? Yes, you do, as we all do. Our willingness to

[46] . "Resilience," *Psychology Today*, https://www.psychologytoday.com/us/basics/resilience.

[47] . "Tolerance," Cambridge Dictionary, https://dictionary.cambridge.org/dictionary/english/tolerance.

see the truth about ourselves by not just seeing the good in us but also the biases, the favoritism, etc. will further help us in our ability to be tolerant of others. By being tolerant, you will eventually expand your circle and allow for connection with other cultures, foods, ideas, and societies. In summary, your life will become richer.

Imagine if Dr. Maya Angelou, at the age of eight, had been conscious of the benefits that she could have reaped from her selective mutism. She had no idea, and yet, she was able to do something: she read, read, and read, which of course led the way to her becoming a great poet and author. This intuitive reaction of living as a selective mute allowed her to survive and cope with this time in her life.

Just imagine what *you* can learn from this time of silence, now that you are conscious of its benefits. Remember, fear really stems from not knowing. However, now you know how much you can learn during your time of silence, so it would be a clever idea not to fear it but to indulge it. Indulging it will allow you to break free from that cage you sing from.

I Know Why the Caged Bird Sings
by Maya Angelou:

…The caged bird sings
With fearful trill
Of things unknown
But longed for still
And his tune is heard
On the distant hill
For the caged bird
Sings of freedom.

Indulge in the silence, contemplate *you*, and decide whether you want to be the caged bird that sings of freedom or the freedom itself that comes when you know who you are and accept that which you are and grow from there.

Unconditional Love for Thee
by Lola Lola

Where have you been when my sadness has crept up without leaving any room for joy?
Where are you right now that I long for and desire unconditional love?
Unconditional love knows no limits, no limits to love,
Love in despair, love in spirit, love unconditional love,
Where are you?
Where are you when I desire you?
Where are you with your mystery, with your vision of perfection?
Where are you with your fairies and angelic and mystical dragonflies?
Where are you with the taboo of Unconditional?

CHAPTER 7

GUILT, SELF-CONCEPT, SELF-ESTEEM

Ask yourself: *What crime have I committed? What has been my offense? What are the facts?* Then repeat to yourself, as many times as possible, the truth:

> I have not committed any crime against anyone. The fact is, I had an experience that I am not to be blamed for, as what does a child know? Children are at the mercy of those around them. What is there for me to feel guilty of? I am a good guy! I am a good gal! I don't hurt anyone and respect all small children. There is absolutely nothing I should be ashamed of. I did not provoke anyone to behave this way toward me. And no one ever, child or not, provokes anyone to behave in this manner to another human being, period.
>
> I am not responsible for the actions of others but only for my own from this moment on. I should not allow myself to feel guilty about anything.

When your self-talks turn to this, you are understanding that you were a victim then, and that as a survivor you can make positive changes in your life regardless of anyone's opinion of you or of those who failed you when you were under their care as a child. Now you are on to something! Now you are focusing your attention on the person who most needs it: yourself.

Now, for old time's sake, let's go over the following concepts that I am sure you have heard numerous times. I know we all know the meaning of them, just like we know the meaning of happiness, yet sometimes we fail, despite our circumstances, to be happy. You know these terms, but have you internalized them, and have you danced to their beat?

SELF-CONCEPT

Self-concept is defined in *The Social Work Dictionary* as the image or picture people have of themselves, including their own identity, body image, personality traits, and evaluation of self (self-esteem).[48]

In addition, Robert Franken indicates that "There is a great deal of research which shows that the self-concept is, perhaps, the basis for all motivated behavior. It is the self-concept that gives rise to possible selves, and it is possible selves that create the motivation for behavior."[49]

SELF-ESTEEM

Franken suggests that self-concept is related to self-esteem in that "People who have good self-esteem have a clearly differentiated self-concept ... *When people know themselves,* they can maximize outcomes because they know what they can and cannot do."[50]

Franken also notes, "There is a growing body of research which indicates that it is possible to change the self-concept. Self-change is not

---

[48] . Robert L. Barker, *The Social Work Dictionary*, 5th reprint ed. (Washington, DC: NASW Press, 2003).

[49] . Quoted in W. Huitt, "Self and Self-Views," *Educational Psychology Interactive* (Valdosta, GA: Valdosta State University, 2011), http://www.edpsycinteractive.org/topics/self/self.html

[50] . Quoted in W. Huitt, "Self and Self-Views."

something that people can but rather it depends on the process of self-reflection. Through *self-reflection*, people often come to view themselves in a new, more powerful way, and it is through this new, more powerful way of viewing the self that people can develop possible selves."[51]

SELF-WORTH

What is your sense of worth? As per the *Social Work Dictionary*,[52] an individual's sense of personal worth is derived more from inner thoughts and values than from praise and recognition from others. Hence, it is important to have a clear knowledge of what constitutes positive versus negative self-talk (as explained in chapter 9) and constantly question and reflect on who you are, what you are, and in what you believe.

Asking the following questions can help you get a clearer view of your overall self-concept and self-esteem:

- What are my values?
- What are my most valued and deeply rooted beliefs, and how do I feel about them?
- What ideas and concepts guide me?
- How many times a day do I look at myself and say how handsome or beautiful I am?
- Do I do self-care, and do I do it for myself or others?
- Am I worth good treatment?
- What is good treatment for me?

Write your answers down and, if necessary, post them, say them, and reflect on them.

To reiterate, to make changes in your self-concept and self-esteem, you need to "know thyself." Thus the need for self-reflection, or what I

---

[51] . Quoted in W. Huitt, "Self and Self-Views."

[52] . Robert L. Barker, *The Social Work Dictionary*, 5th reprint ed. (Washington, DC: NASW Press, 2003).

like to call *self-cleaning*. Recognize what step you are in and know that there is nothing for you to feel guilty or ashamed about.

Evaluating how this feeling of guilt can impact your overall self-concept and self-esteem is imperative to your process of finding the way to a better you. The individual or individuals who perpetrated this act should feel guilty for violating you, not you. When people who have been so profoundly hurt continue to find excuses for what others did to them, it's because deep down, they are truly the most caring and lovable individuals, and they are just not aware of how much they continue to revictimize themselves when engaging in this kind of behavior. Then, as a result, they continue with a sense of guilt, sometimes for the remainder of their time in this world.

Louise Thorton wrote, "A growing child gains self-esteem and confidence from the value placed upon her by adults whom she trusts and upon whom she must depend. The sexually exploited child, however, rarely elicits a reaction necessary to promote a positive identity. Unsupported in her right to be protected, to be angry, or to express justified indignation, she feels she deserves no more than to be sexually used." She adds, "When the offense remains hidden, unanswered, and unchallenged, the sexuality, the very biology of the offended child, becomes her shame."[53] Though these quotes refer to a female victim of sexual abuse, I want to point out that the same applies to a male victim.

My belief is that guilt comes from the shame developed mainly due to the wonderful human being you are. Yes, the wonderful human being you are! You were sexually abused as a child more than likely by an individual who you felt love for—a stepfather, uncle, teacher, mother, father, perhaps a grandparent. However, on top of this, you basically take on a built-in feeling of guilt, almost as if saying, "The guilt or shame you never felt, I will place on myself."

It is as if you have an unconscious need to pay for something you have not done. You are in the prison of your own mind, with feelings

---

[53] . Louise Thorton and Ellen Bass 1991, *I Never Told Anyone*: writings by women survivors of child sexual abuse, page 13. First Harper Perennial edition published 1991.

about something you're not guilty of and don't need to feel shameful about. When will you break the chains and walk, head up and facing the sun, out of that prison? You were vulnerable to the adults around you. You depended on them for protection. You were betrayed by them. So what is there for you to feel guilty about? Why the shame? Feelings of guilt and shame will lead you to develop an extremely poor opinion of yourself, which then leads you to having a vague self-concept and nonexistent self-esteem. Now you are not a vulnerable child but an adult willing and responsible to restore the broken pieces by placing them back were they needed to be in the first place.

In the Japanese tradition called *kintsugi*, meaning "golden repair," they use liquid gold, silver, or lacquer and add a golden powder when putting pottery together that was previously broken. The idea behind the kintsugi tradition is not to hide the scars but reveal them so as to identify part of the history of the pot, which will further serve to increase its value. This philosophy is similar to *wabi-sabi* which embraces the imperfect and/or defective. What we can summarize from this is that we are even more of value with flaws and experiences than we would be without them. This is reason enough to embrace our experiences—the good and the apparent bad—which will facilitate a positive self-concept and overall renewed self-esteem.

If we are not careful, our negative self-talk and poor self-concept/self-esteem become a vicious cycle, going round and round, that only a limited number of individuals can pull out of because of the amount of inner work it actually entails. Will you be one of those who identify where they are and continue their journey to becoming a thriving individual? Pulling out of feelings of guilt, shame, or disgust will be a challenge, but it is one worth pursuing. You will grow through much pain, as for any individual, having experienced abuse or not, it is a painful process to have the courage to recognize that we are not the perfect or righteous individuals we perceive ourselves to be. It takes courage to embrace the real us.

What picture do you have of yourself? Place a picture of yourself on a nearby mirror where you can look at it to further evaluate your body image and speak out or internalize your positive traits in your ongoing effort to evaluate yourself.

CONCLUSION OF SELF-ESTEEM

I personally like the idea that self-esteem is strongly associated with consciousness. Consciousness is simply *being* or *becoming aware of.* On the lines below, write about negative feelings associated to any trauma or event you have not come to terms with.

_____

_____

_____

_____

_____

_____

_____

For me, it is simply becoming aware of who you are and not denying what you went through, bringing it to total consciousness, and learning how that impacts not just others but your internal and external world. I believe this sets the stage for your future success in life—whatever you may define as success. This is why in our healing process or in our way to be thriving individuals, it is so important to recognize that you were a victim (which reminds you that you have nothing to feel guilty about), and then to recognize yourself as a survivor (a person who was able to endure this and continues to function within society, understanding that perhaps you have some misconceptions that you need to work on).

By taking these first steps, you have now become conscious that yes, you were victimized by someone you had no control over. At the same time, you recognize that you should not feel guilty and can eventually have control over this. During this process, you start looking at the fact that you are surviving daily. Now you start giving credit to yourself, which is a start toward changing distorted thinking patterns and building on overall self-respect, self-concept, and self-esteem. See how it all comes together! Recognizing you are a victim and eventually moving on from this will change your life altogether to great accomplishment, and your love for yourself will be so great that you cannot even imagine. The happiness and inner freedom that awaits you is indescribable.

In summary, when you truly challenge yourself and become conscious (self-aware) of what happened to you and to what extent this changed your life, you can possibly be reborn in spirit and even transcend. And as we've discussed in this chapter, your spirit is your force within that gives the body life, energy, and power. This state of awareness is *awesome*, because now you get to make decisions that will work in your favor, with the determination to change that with which you are not satisfied. Now you are the one walking your own walk and asking:

- Did this experience change my life for the worse or for the better?
- Will I let my perpetrator get the best of me?
- What scars left by this experience do I need to continue carrying with me and why?
- In how many ways do I keep making excuses to not truly do the things I want to do?

How many more years are you willing to waste?

In my mind, every time I see former victims of severe sexual abuse, such as Oprah Winfrey and Maya Angelou, with a smile, thriving daily, and attempting to help others, I see self-victory. I see that all things are possible if you believe in yourself. I see the possibility of changing any negative experience to a positive one. I do not see survival, I see *thriving*, which is a whole different phenomenon.

There are millions and millions of individuals still in the dark about the importance of understanding our true role in our healing/thriving process. It is not what others do but what we do for ourselves that will have profound significance in the long run. And as a result, we should not have any excuses. I do not mean to sound tragic, yet I do believe that for humanity's sake, we have a responsibility to make this world a better place. And how do we make this world a better place? Yes, one step at a time. Start at home; start with *you* first! You are home and your home needs sweeping, love, compassion, remodeling, etc.

It is my belief that Gandhi, whom I deeply appreciated for his attempt to give a message of love and insisting that change was possible with his uncompromising refusal to engage in violence, firmly informed us by his actions of the importance of knowing who you are, coming to terms with that, being true to yourself first, and being persistent in your mission for change. If Gandhi taught us anything, for me, it is the importance of becoming conscious of who we are and how we impact ourselves, others, and the world around us. And that alone should set the stage for change for any individual.

The tools so far presented as identifying what step you are in, or writing, are just tools to use in your healing process and, ultimately, in getting to know yourself. Gandhi's life story repeatedly emphasizes our responsibility to our own self. We are not responsible for the way of life chosen by any adults around us, only for our own.

Gandhi was born in Porbandar, India, on October 2, 1869, and was assassinated on January 30, 1948. Gandhi was a spiritual and political leader. He was the Father of India in the freedom struggle and independence movement. Gandhi spent approximately twenty-one years in South Africa practicing law, where he adopted the Satyagraha to fight the racist regime. He returned to India in 1915 and continued his fight for peace and freedom. The Satyagraha movement was a nonviolent way of protesting against injustices and was also adopted by Martin Luther King Jr.[54, 55]

This does not mean that we don't need others to help us on our journey. We are definitely social creatures, and the more support, unconditional love, and understanding we have, the better our outcome. Yet for now, during this self-cleaning process, your main responsibility is to give support, love, unconditional love, and understanding to yourself. Eventually, all that you are doing for yourself now will inevitably rub off on others.

So, if you are like me, with an internal need to be present in people's lives and help them transition to a better, more fulfilled role, then for the time being, remember that you can only give that which you have at the moment. It is time to gather all those tools being provided to you and to recognize that you are a survivor ready to become an accomplisher. You will strive, eventually arriving at what you want most, and that it is to be a thriving individual.

Continue to *ask, ask, ask*! What do you expect from yourself? What do you expect from those around you? In the meantime, and for the long run, I suggest that you do not expect, just do. Work, accept, acknowledge, but don't expect anything from anyone. It is no one's responsibility but your own to create your path to making your dreams come true. You are an adult now, responsible for yourself. Remember to practice being nice to yourself.

[54]. Abhishek Bansal, "Mahatma Gandhi Was Thrown Off Train in South Africa," inshorts (August 13, 2006), https://inshorts.com/en/news/mahatma-gandhi-was-thrown-off-train-in-south-africa-1471093415623.
[55]. "Mahatma Gandhi's Satyagraha Movement," Maps of India, www.mapsofindia.com/personalities/gandhi/satyagarh.html.

CHAPTER 8
DEPRESSION AND THE BUILDING OF BRIDGES

Depression is a common aftermath of child sexual abuse. That is why it is important to build bridges. In this chapter, we will briefly discuss the definition of *depression* and the risks of developing symptoms when you have been a victim of sexual abuse.

On the website of the American Counseling Association, Melissa Hall and Joshua Hall write that "depression has been found to be the most common long-term symptoms among survivors."[56] According to researchers J. N. Briere and D. M. Elliot, adult survivors of child sexual abuse have a four times greater lifetime risk of developing major depression compared with people who do not have an abuse history.[57]

The following list is a review of the symptoms of depression and how suicide is a common factor associated with depression:[58]

- difficulty concentrating, remembering details, and making decisions
- fatigue and decreased energy
- feelings of guilt, worthlessness, and/or helplessness

---

[56] . Melissa Hall and Joshua Hall, Article 19, https://www.counseling.org/docs/default-source/vistas/vistas_2011_article_19.pdf?sfvrsn=144ec071_11, page 2.

[57] . J. N. Briere and D. M. Elliot, "Immediate and Long-Term Impacts of Child Sexual Abuse," *The Future of Children* 4, no. 2 (Summer/Fall 1994), https://dpi.wi.gov/sites/default/files/imce/sspw/pdf/inspireimpacts_csa.pdf.

[58] . Debra Fulghum Bruce, PhD, "What Is Depression?" WebMD (2002), https://www.webmd.com/depression/guide/detecting-depression.

- feeling of hopelessness and/or pessimism
- insomnia, early-morning wakefulness, or excessive sleeping
- irritability, restlessness
- loss of interest in activities or hobbies once pleasurable, including sex
- overeating or appetite loss
- persistent aches or pains, headaches, cramps, or digestive problems that do not ease even with treatment
- persistent sad, anxious, or "empty" feelings
- thoughts of suicide, suicide attempts
- a sudden switch from being incredibly sad to being very calm or appearing to be happy (most of the time the reason for this being that in suicide the individual may have found a solution to their problem)
- always talking or thinking about death
- clinical depression (deep sadness, loss of interest, trouble sleeping and eating) that gets worse
- having a "death wish," tempting fate by taking risks that could lead to death, such as driving through red lights
- losing interest in things one used to care about
- making comments about being hopeless, helpless, or worthless
- putting affairs in order, tying up loose ends, changing a will
- saying things like "It would be better if I wasn't here" or "I want out"
- talking about suicide (killing oneself)
- visiting or calling people one cares about

I suggest you develop keen eyesight or "an eye of an eagle," an idiom used by many to recognize whether at any time in your life you have experienced or are experiencing symptoms of depression. When it comes to you and your mental health, you are the only one who has the responsibility of watching out for *you* and taking the necessary measures to prevent a mental illness or have a mental illness worsen.

Sexual abuse and mental illness are still taboo subjects—subjects that most of us are afraid to talk about but yet they still happen. We have a preconceived idea that if we do not talk about these things, they will not happen, or better yet, they will go away. And I suggest the reverse: we *have* to talk about it. We have to talk about child sexual abuse, postpartum depression, bipolar disorder, schizophrenia, just as we talk about the food we eat or the brand of clothes we like to buy. By not acknowledging this and the struggle lived by many who experience the aftermath of sexual abuse or living with a mental illness, how can we find the courage to fight against it and to work more on preventing mental illness or child sexual abuse?

How do you do this? By becoming aware of the symptoms of depression, knowing the different treatment modalities, and allowing yourself to be humble enough to ask for help if you think it is necessary. This will win you more than half the battle with depression. As with any mental illness left untreated, depression will have devastating effects to your life. This is vital to your overall well-being, and at the end of the day, it will make way for you to live that life of fulfillment that you so wish for.

Remember that everything is interrelated: guilt, shame, your innocence being taken away. All the defense mechanisms you use are, in my opinion, the result of your unconscious fight with depression. Therefore, for now and for the purposes of this guide, it will be good just to have in mind the following definition of what constitutes depression and the main question you should be asking yourself.

As James Hollis put it, "Think of what the word means literally, to de-press, to press down. What is 'pressed down'? Life's energy, life's intentionality, life's teleology is pressed down, thwarted, denied, violated … Life is warring against life. For 'life's energy, life's intentionality, life's teleology' to be pressed down or thwarted means for me in some fundamental sense to not be allowing who I really am to emerge. I need to explore the unique situations and things in my individual story where that is occurring. What in me is keeping me back?"[59]

---

[59] . "Listening to Our Depression" from lawyerswithdepression.com, April 10, 2008, https://www.printfriendly.com/p/g/mB23nt.

Hollis is a Jungian psychoanalyst, author of seventeen books, and responsible for the *Soul Heal* documentary.[60] It is interesting that, in the quote above, he writes, "Life's energy, life's intentionality, life's teleology is pressed down, thwarted, denied, violated." Well, you have been denied your rights, you have been pressed down, and you have been violated. Now turn it around and ask yourself this: *Up to when am I going to continue pressing down and denying myself the right to follow my dreams? When will I stop violating my own right for respect, love, courage, dignity, success, and a good standing within society?* As Hollis suggests you ask, "What in me is keeping me back?"

When you finally decide to ask yourself this question, you are consciously holding yourself accountable for how you will live your life from this moment on. In each of our lives, there does come a time when we, independently of what we have been through or on whom the fault lies, must take responsibility for ourselves and our actions. Once you have decided to finally take responsibility for your actions, feelings, thoughts, or present situation, rest assured you will find yourself stuck asking the following questions:

- What will I do?
- When will I start working on myself?
- How will I start?
- What steps am I taking to get where I want to go?
- When will I stop pressing myself down?

By identifying what step you're on, you are emphasized as the most important in this guide, as it is a method to go to the root, to the core of your present situation, to pinpoint the origin of where you need to start picking up the broken pieces of the puzzle.

In his book *The Soul of a Citizen: Living with Conviction in a Cynical Time*, Paul Rogat Loeb wrote, "Again and again, I've heard active citizens say that what motivates them the most is the desire to respect what they see in the mirror. The exercise isn't about vanity, but about

---

[60] . https://www.jameshollis.net/.

values, about taking stock of ourselves and comparing the convictions we say we hold with the lives we lead. It's about seeing ourselves from the viewpoint of our communities, the earth, maybe even God. If eyes are the windows to the soul, and faces are reflections of character, looking in the mirror lets us step back from the flux of our lives and hold ourselves accountable."[61]

And yes, we need to hold ourselves accountable in every aspect of our lives, including our mental health. We need to watch out for ourselves, remembering that if I'm OK, you're OK. However, that said, an individual is also responsible for discarding any biological reasons for depression and should seek medical attention along with taking necessary steps for their healing process as described in this guide.

You should be aware that individuals completely responsible for themselves would benefit from taking a more comprehensive approach to their overall well-being, and like that bring a sense of balance to what constitutes their nutrition, level of exercise, work, school, family, and leisure activities. Likewise, they would increase the overall opportunity for individual growth mentally, physically, and spiritually.

BUILDING BRIDGES

Ask yourself, "In this situation, am I building or breaking a bridge?" Why the need to build bridges? Why is answering this question so important for you at your present moment and in the meeting of your future successes? This question emphasizes the need to accept or seek help from others whether you like it or not. You are not an island, and rest assured, you will need help from others. Being humble enough to ask for help can be an opportunity to gain experience and grow.

During your process toward healing, you will face many challenges. The greatest one is confronting yourself and asking, "In this situation, am I building or breaking a bridge?" Learning to always keep your doors

---

[61] . Paul Rogat Loeb, *The Soul of a Citizen: Living with Conviction in a Cynical Time* (New York: St. Martin Press, 1999), 14.

open and treating everyone you meet with love and respect regardless of who they are or their economic status will be of benefit to you in the short and in the long run, as you never know what help you will need or who will provide it.

Thus, it is important to keep our humility when it is needed, and always within context. When it comes to helping yourself grow, you need courage and persistence, not modesty. You need modesty to build bridges; what you need for yourself is some tough love.

You need to function within a society that needs you as well. If someone does not treat you as you deserve, let them go. Most of the time, people don't react to us but to their internal war; thus, use modesty. Let it go and continue to build that bridge regardless of them. But for yourself, practice tough love and keep an eagle eye to not engage in anything that can deter you from your path, such as anger toward others or negative self-talk or going back to the common hideouts already discussed.

Use the resources presented to you in this guide to build the bridge within. Envision the resources as the pieces of wood to be used for building the bridge between your point of identification and the arrival of the thriving you. Your resources are the pieces of wood placed to help you walk through every step of the way toward guiding you out of the internal turmoil to the thriving you.

If, despite your endless effort to keep a door open, it closes, then practice saying goodbye, turning around, and walking away. Focus on your internal war and accept it, make peace with it, and continue to build your internal bridges, which usually get built when you finally start accepting and loving your own self.

You can be absolutely sure that 100 percent of the time, that which we give comes back to us, and usually tripled. So build, don't destroy. Start with building yourself. Build that bridge between your mind, your heart, and your community, as they need unity to function properly.

Well, now you may be asking, "Great, Lola Lola, and how do you expect me to do this?" Let's briefly look at some bridge-building tools.

Patience

You have probably heard this so many times, but it is imperative that you really understand that Rome was not built in a day. Don't be hard on yourself and remember that it takes time to heal. Just as the song says, it takes time to heal a broken heart. Your body, heart, mind, and soul, and spirit need time—yet remember, not stagnation.

Discretion

Be aware that building bridges does not mean building bridges with people or circumstances that do not serve you anymore. When in the face of adversity and with situations, people, and events that may work to deter you from your attempt to reach the point of thriving, just walk away. Turn around and leave immediately.

Remember the meaning of depression: "pressing down." Automatically, you recognize this can't possibly be good for you and will distract you from your long-term goal, which is to learn how to thrive. What do you do then? You leave immediately, no questions asked, no excuses. Politely make your way toward the company of optimists.

Optimism/Humor/Positive Outlook

Robert Brault defines an optimist as "Someone who figures that taking a step backward after taking a step forward is not a disaster, it's a cha cha."[62] So, cha cha your way to thriving!

I met Lillian Monterrey, an international motivational speaker and author of the book *Follow Your Instincts: A Self-Discovery for Personal Empowerment*, at a book convention many years ago. She may not recall me, nor can I remember the name of the convention or book fair. However, I do remember what she told me that day.

---

[62] . The Quotable Coach, https://www.thequotablecoach.com/optimist-someone-who-figures-that-taking-a-step-backward/#:~:text=%E2%80%9COptimist%3A%20Someone%20who%20figures%20that%20taking%20a%20step,a%20part%20in%20the%20magnificent%20miracle%20of%20living.

I had asked her how to write a book, as it has always been my dream to write one, and she suddenly handed me her card (which I keep in my wallet to this very day) and asked, "How do you bring down an elephant?"

Well, I can tell you that I stood there looking as if I had just seen a one-eyed Martian. She anticipated that response and answered for me: "With one pinch at a time."

For approximately fifteen years, that was all I had to work with. I was always making way for the company of optimism one pinch at a time. Some days were significantly painful, but still I managed to find a way to stay close to optimism. And now here we are, working toward the thriving individual "one pinch at a time."

Overall, optimism is a general expectancy that at the end of it all, everything will work out for the best despite the current situation. An optimist will have the tendency to see the glass as half full, versus the pessimist's tendency to see the glass as half empty. A more hopeful view for present and future situations/outcomes is the norm. This can act as an intrinsic motivator toward continuous efforts at self-reflection to ultimately become the best version of yourself.

During this challenging journey to find the thriving you, get in the habit, especially during tough situations, of asking yourself whether the glass is half full or half empty. This will be another key tool to help you move forward with your plans. The optimist is a better side to pick, and one that will encourage you to never give up. However, remember that remaining on the side of optimism is easy when all is going smoothly. When it is not, you will need to muster much courage to remain optimistic.

Then, like Les Brown[63] would say, when Murphy's Law pays you a visit, you can have a few sayings in your SYAF (Save Your Ass File) to stay optimistic. These sayings can ease the daily struggle of being you

---

[63] . Motivational Speaker Les Brown, https://www.bing.com/videos/riverview/relatedvideo?q=les+brown+and+story+about+murphys+law&mid=928B7B17606C0DD3BD4E928B7B17606C0DD3BD4E.

and help you refocus on your short- and long-term goals, one pinch or day at a time.

Laughing Matters

In addition, you can always add humor to your life. Remember Dr. Patch Adams? Patch Adams, born May 28, 1945, was an American physician, social activist, clown, and author. He founded The Gesundheit! Institute in 1971 and devoted thirty years to changing America's healthcare system. He believes that laughter, joy, and creativity are an integral part of the healing process. Therefore, he believes that true health care must incorporate laughter, joy, and creativity.[64]

Dr. Patch Adams devoted his life to the study of what makes people happy. He believes that "the most revolutionary act one can commit in our world is to be happy." And I second that!

Why incorporate laughter as a tool? Well, because laughter has the tendency to lighten your struggles and, if used wisely, helps you maintain an attitude of hope even through situations that you may unfortunately have no explanation for. Now you have two friends to keep on your side during your ride: humor/laughter and optimism.

Furthermore, remaining on the side of the optimist daily is a challenge in and of itself. Therefore, it is imperative that you always have a plan that allows you to get back on your feet when the bad days come. These sayings are part of my plan A to get back on track. You can use these or collect your own sayings according to what you know will work for you. In the meantime, I share with you some that have worked for me repeatedly and that I find funny as well.

- **Whatever tickles your pickle**: This is my number-one expression. It can be thought of as obscene, but in my mind, the pickle is the other person's idea, problem, or concern that is not mine. In addition, it is also an opportunity to laugh by adding humor. *Love it!* (Learned it from both my daughters.)

---

[64] . The Gesundheit! Institute, http://patchadams.org.

- **Whatever!**: This helps in times of stress. It is funny and gives you a chance to mentally relax, as whatever is just that … *whatever*. Sometimes, you need to relax and say *whatever*. Or, as in the film starring Tom Cruise, *Risky Business*, "Sometimes you have to say *what the f———*." In our case, *whatever* sounds a little better, right? But whatever tickles your pickle!

- **OK!**: OK is OK. Remember, if I'm OK, you're OK. So, start by saying it's OK, I'm OK, everybody is OK, you're OK, they're OK. Today, regardless of my circumstances, I am OK.

- **Oh well!**: I learned to say this early in my career with my first true work supervisor within the psychology field. Every time she would see an error in my writing, I would say, "Oh, Maritza, I made a mistake." And she would say, "Oh well, here, do it again." I would get upset, but this is life. You make a mistake? Oh well, do it again. The more mistakes we make, the better; the more we end up learning, and the better we will be at what we are. The harder the teacher or the criticism, the better you will be at the end. So don't worry and don't get mad, just fix it. Oh well, do it again!

- **One day/one pinch**: This is just one day. Tomorrow will come soon, but today is today. It is one day at a time. Little by little, one day at a time, you will get to where you want to be: thriving. Remember in the first *Annie* movie when she sings, "Tomorrow, tomorrow, you're only a day away"? Tomorrow is tomorrow. Focus on today while always keeping your hopes up for tomorrow, as it is only a day away. The sun will come out tomorrow for all of us; you are not going to be left out. At least not on your watch.

- **There is no way to go but up**: My mentor, friend, and former field instructor at Florida International University, in the social work department, who passed away some time ago, told me once when I was doubting whether I would pursue my degree within the social work or psychology field at a master's level that "There is no way to go but up." At this time, I was also a bit disappointed with the mental health system. I was torn about continuing my degree in psychology on the master's level, as I had just completed my bachelor's in psychology. My former mentor passed away due to cancer, but she is still here with me, as it is her voice I hear telling me that "There is no way to go but up" when doubt comes troubling in.

It was her encouragement that gave me the determination to complete my master's degree, and her voice is behind all my successes. She continues to remind me daily that "There is no way to go but up." Still today, I keep her post up reminding me of this. Which, interestingly enough, if you further analyze, is closely associated with the meaning of optimism.

- *"Good morning, this is God. I will be handling all your business today."*: This comes from a former colleague and devoted friend who also passed away due to breast cancer. She was the first true colleague who had an influence on my life. We met when I arrived at my first day of work and went to sit down to what was going to be my first real work desk as a comprehensive diagnostic evaluator (all I could find as a psychology major at the moment, never realizing that it would be the place I would ever love the most). I was twenty-five years old and already had a child. On my desk, I saw a little note left by this colleague saying, "Good morning, this is God. I will be handling all your business today."

From that moment on, at every job I've had, I write this note and put it on my desk to remind me that I am not alone, and you will be amazed how this little note can change any situation. God and the angels are with me constantly, making way for me to win my battles at the end of it all (again, optimism). As

101

my colleague used to say, "Wonderful." She would say this no matter what her circumstance.

So, whatever! Whatever tickles your pickle! Oh well! Wonderful! Good morning, this is God. I will be handling all your business today! There is no way to go but up! One day/one pinch! OK! Whatever!

CHAPTER 9

MIND TRICKS AND RECOMMENDATIONS

I n this chapter, I'll give you more tools, mind tricks, and strategies that can help you daily to refocus (one pinch/one day at a time) on your own process of meeting your set objectives, and ultimately meeting the long-term goals that encompass meeting the thriving you.

TRICKS

Reading

Read autobiographies of individuals who, despite their obstacles, have thrived or continue to thrive daily to make their dreams come true. Read about Abraham Lincoln, for example, who fought for what he believed in (civil rights), making many of his dreams come true despite all the obstacles, including his struggle with major depression. Read about others briefly mentioned in this book, such as Maya Angelou and Oprah Winfrey. Read books by Dr. Wayne Dyer, Iyanla Vanzant, and many, many more. Michael Oher is an excellent example of how you can thrive despite anything, including abandonment by those who are supposed to be the most influential figures in your life.

No matter what kind of bad experience you have had, all individuals who at the end of their journey find themselves thriving will one day make a conscious choice to accept who and what they were or are and somehow align themselves with their true inner being, making way for a transforming change in their life that leads them to become their best self. When I say "accept who and what they were or are," I mean to admit the truth of who you are, and what scars your experience left you with. It means not denying your hurt, your truth, but then being able to say, "OK, this happened to me, but this terrible experience will not define me. It will not destroy me. It will not leave me in a bed depressed. It will not take my life. I will learn from this experience and become a better person."

Always keep in mind that these changes will take effect one day at a time. Therefore, it is important that you are benevolent with yourself in your journey. Practice compassion, but don't forget the importance of personal tough love.

Dancing and Movement

Dance and body movement combined with deep breathing exercises can be an exceptional therapy and stress reducer. They can be done behind closed doors and in the privacy of your home. One practiced by me for the past twenty years or so—so I can attest to its benefits—is to put on your favorite song and move to its rhythm. Cry, laugh, visualize yourself somewhere you love, talk to those who hurt you, thank those who really love you, find the peace you are looking for. All the while, keep dancing and taking deep breaths. Fill yourself with new energy to continue in your journey.

Listening to Music

Carefully choose the music you listen to. Try to listen to music that inspires, motivates, or heals you. Pick music that gives a message of hope, courage, and love. Surround yourself with positivity. People say that we are what we eat, and I say we are also what we listen to daily, as well as who we hang around with, what are daily habits are, and what we say to ourselves daily. That is why people who value positivity, optimism, and humor can be great friends to have around, not just during your journey but throughout your life.

Picking a Mantra

Yolimba, an acquaintance from Skype, introduced me to this mantra she had for herself that goes something like this: *Whatever the situation, I will beat it; it will not beat me.* For example, "I will beat this test, it will not beat me." Write it down, post it, sing it, dance to it.

Setting Daily Goals

Make sure you are doing something about it *daily*. No excuses. It can be something as simple as writing on the bathroom mirror a little reminder of things to accomplish for the day, week, month or even year.

Taking Time for Yourself

Take fifteen minutes to an hour daily just for yourself. Make sure this time is only for you. Take a walk; read a book; go to the movies; give yourself a flower. Try to choose films that give messages of strength, courage, love, etc. Talk to a good friend. Go and be around people who make you happy and show they respect you. Always remember that those friends who show you respect are the ones who genuinely love you.

Talking It Out

If in need, talk to someone you trust who understands you. Seek help when in need, and don't be ashamed. Remember: faces we see, but hearts we don't. You never know what an individual holds inside, what that person has gone through, and what that person can teach you. So, talk. Express yourself always with someone you trust and who will respect and maintain the privacy of your conversations.

Making a Name for Yourself

This may sound odd, but make a name for yourself that has meaning to you—a nickname like, for example, Lola Lola (a name I have always loved and thus created for myself). Be aware that people may criticize you, but hey, remember that it is you who needs to work on yourself. It is about *you*, not them.

This new name will represent all the positive characteristics you want to be associated with until, little by little, you become them, such as happy, confident, ambitious, loyal, honest, loving to all people around you, wanting to help your community, wanting to see things clearly, wanting to help others be the best that can be, wanting to build positive interpersonal relationships, not being part of any violence, and advocating for human rights.

One good example of this is Iyanla Vanzant. She was born in Brooklyn, New York, in the back of a taxicab to an alcoholic mother, the result of an extramarital affair. Iyanla's mother died when she was two, and she was left under the care of her father, who was both emotionally and physically not present in her life for the most part. It would be customary for her father to leave her under the care of different relatives, including an uncle who raped her at age nine.

Iyanla's original name is Rhonda Harris. After many trials and tribulations, including raising three children and surviving domestic violence and two suicide attempts, Iyanla was able to go to school and get a degree as summa cum laude, then continue to pursue a degree in law from the law school at City University of New York. Thanks to her excellent oratory skills and published books, she spreads her message of hope to many. She has won awards and recognition throughout her mission to bring hope to people's lives.

In an interview with Oprah,[65] Rhonda or Iyanla talked about why she changed her name between the ages of twenty-eight and twenty-nine. Iyanla explained that the life she was living was not *her*. Rhonda represented the survivor—a resourceful, broken, wounded, sorrowful woman. Iyanla changed her name to symbolize letting go of the much-abused Rhonda Harris. But she said that "had it not been for her, I would not be sitting here today." She added, "I would not have survived the

---

[65] . Super Soul Sunday: How Iyanla Vanzant Chose Her Own Name, Oprah Winfrey Network, YouTube, https://www.youtube.com/watch?v=oudvnw3wXls.

abuse, the abandonment, the rejection." Iyanla represents the mother/ teacher, and Iyanla states that "teaching is her mission."

Being Yourself

We are all unique individuals, and what works for one person may not necessarily work for another. Thus, develop your own strategies and mind tricks and add them to this list. I am sure that in your journey and where you find yourself now, you also have individuals, such as the ones mentioned in this guide, to help you to never give up. Write down what they told you that inspired change in you.

Observe what you do in those moments when you are being your best self and do more of that. What is it you do, and who is around? What makes you *you*? There is nothing better than being you and maintaining friends such as optimism and humor. Positivity, optimism, and humor will always work in your favor, so do not ever let them go. Write your mind tricks down, say them, sing them, post them, gossip them, dance to their beat. *Dare to let go and thrive daily!*

TOOLS

Understand that all of the steps, techniques, and tips that have previously been given all invite you to do some cognitive restructuring, stemming from cognitive theory. Definitions of the following terms were taken from the *Dictionary of Social Work* by Robert L. Baker:

I. "But first what is Cognition? What is this? It is the process by which we understand, remember, and evaluate information."

II. Cognitive Theory: A general idea about the ways in which individuals develop their intellectual capacity for receiving, processing, and behaving on information. Cognitive theory focuses attention on behavior and how it is determined by thinking and goal determination, versus particularly the result of instinctive drives or unconscious motivations.

III. Cognitive Behavior Therapies (CBT): Generally, focuses on the present and emphasizes looking at a person's thoughts, feelings, and behaviors with the main idea to work on replacing negative thoughts with more positive ones. Main goal being changing the behaviors that are causing chaos or difficulty in our lives, keeping us from reaching our true potential in life.

IV. Cognitive Restructuring: Procedure used to change negative or unrealistic thoughts or attributions to more positive ones. Baker defines it as, "Psychotherapy technique designed to reveal faulty logic in the client's pattern of thinking and to help the client replace those patterns with rational and logical thinking."[66]

Cognitive restructuring is closely related to the idea of changing our own negative self-talk to a more positive tone, in that the focus is on becoming increasingly aware of our automatic thoughts and to assess how positive or negative they really are. Cognitive restructuring suggests that you notice your negative thoughts and assess how these negative thoughts may be keeping you from reaching your most desired goals, such as having better interpersonal relationships, being more benevolent to yourself, and being more optimistic about life in general or in the becoming of a thriving you.

Generally, cognitive restructuring suggests that you restructure or restore your thoughts to more positive ones.[67] You reframe your negative thoughts to thoughts that work for you and not against you. You take a moment to observe those thoughts as if you were watching a soccer game at a distance. By watching at a distance, you will more than likely have the energy and time to change the play, and the same goes with your thoughts. By you changing your negative thoughts to more positive ones, you change the game and, just like that, are more likely to increase your incidence of success.

Having positive affirmations for each negative thought, choosing of

---

[66] . Robert L. Barker, *The Social Work Dictionary*, 5th reprint ed. (Washington, DC: NASW Press, 2003), 79-80.

[67] . Robert L. Barker, *The Social Work Dictionary*, 5th reprint ed. (Washington, DC: NASW Press, 2003), 79-80.

optimism, and developing mind tricks are all ways to change negative thoughts that do not serve you anymore. Most of the time, when we stop to take notice of what we say to ourselves daily, we see that what we really say to ourselves is pretty darn mean and can definitely take a toll in our life.

For example, let's say you started to observe the automatic negative thoughts that come to your brain, and you notice that every time you cook a meal, you think, *I hate cooking. I will never be any good at this*, because several times in the past you burned your meal. Well, what will probably happen is that you will not give cooking a meal a chance, and your wish to cook a nice meal for your significant other will never come to be.

However, let's say you notice this negative thought about your meal and replace it with, *I know cooking is not my forte; however, I will try again with a simpler meal in which there are fewer ingredients, and I will look to see if I can find a simple recipe online, as I know I can cook a nice simple meal.* Then, your chances of cooking a simple, nice, delicious meal for your significant other is more likely to happen.

Another example would be thinking, *I am total failure and stupid because I did not pass this English test*, when instead, you could think, *Next time, before I take this test, I will study harder. I know I can pass it if I take time to really study.* You are not stupid; you just need to study harder.

This guide is, in simple terms, attempting to alert you to the benefits that cognitive restructuring can bring to your life, such as decreasing the inaccurate, negative, self-limiting interpretations developed because of your terrible experience with sexual abuse. This is the reason for the emphasis on recognizing that you were a victim of sexual abuse as a child (a time in which you were developing), which may have left you with some cognitive distortions about life and people in general— distortions that may continue to keep you from becoming the thriving individual you know deep inside you were meant to be.

The number-one step of recognizing that you were a victim, before you make any kind of commitment of change for yourself, is imperative. By recognizing you were a victim, you are also accepting yourself and internally saying, *OK, well, there are a few ideas that I have about life, me, and others that may not be correct.* Once you recognize this as being possible, you can make connections as to how your behaviors have been a response to your perceptions, thus allowing for a sense of humility on your part and a willingness to start making changes that will help you live a more fulfilled life.

The emphasis on the use of tools in this guide is essential. Imagine going to a construction site, or to remodel a home or a bathroom, without your tools, such as a drill, ladder, crowbar, measuring tape, screwdriver, putty knife, concrete mixer, and step stool. As a construction worker, you need tools and materials to help you start and complete your goal. Without its fin, the Japanese puffer fish (white-spotted puffer fish) cannot attract its mate. Without pots, cutting boards, or knives, a chef cannot cook, and without knowledge of food chemistry, different cooking styles, historical chefs, and their roots, the opportunities to thrive as a chef may be diminished. Thus, having your tools identified and ready for use is necessary in your willingness to continue toward becoming the thriving individual you wish to be.

The knowledge of different therapies and/or the ability to identify the best coping strategies to use on your path—such as replacing negative self-talk and behaviors with more positive and optimistic ones; immediately recognizing when you may be walking away from your most enduring friends, like humor, positivity, and optimism; and having your mind tricks, strategies, sayings, and mantras either written, recorded, or posted nearby—is a must. Like a writer who needs paper and pen, you need your mind tricks, your best coping mechanisms, and knowledge of different coping strategies. With that said, you need to always have a plan A, B, and C.

In addition, keep in mind the benefits that you can get from:

- creating the habit of observing others around you and learning how they continue to thrive daily
- making it a habit to ask, ask, ask
- reaping the benefits of silence

- informing yourself about what mental illness is
- building bridges (internally as well as with others)
- doing your math psychology calculations

In other words, going to your essence, to the root of where it all started, yet with the necessary tools or resources to thrive.

CHAPTER 10

ZERO TOLERANCE

WHAT CHILDREN SHOULD KNOW: A MESSAGE TO PARENTS

An unknown author once wrote, "A child is a person to carry on what you have started. He is going to sit where you are sitting and when you are gone, attend to those things, which you think are important. You may adopt all the policies you please, but how they are carried out depends on him. He will assume control of cities, states, and nations. He is going to move in and take over your churches, schools, universities, and corporations … The fate of humanity in his hands."[68]

I agree with the above definition of what a child constitutes. In my opinion, this definition clearly explains the importance of protecting our children. It can serve to remind us of the importance of practicing prevention and having zero tolerance for any type of abuse toward children. *Prevention* holds the key, as it is far better and easier to prevent than to ameliorate an unpleasant situation.

Therefore, education is the key once more. Parents must first take an active role in educating themselves to then be able to educate their children not just in academics but in how they are to protect themselves in a world in which abuse is possible and rampant. I advise parents to talk the real talk. The only way children will learn to protect themselves is to be educated in clear, simple terms, and in an age-appropriate way, using the actual terms. Children will not be traumatized by using what I

---

[68] . U.S. Dept.: HHS, OHDS, 1984.

call "the real terms" but will be from falling victim to horrendous acts in which their sense of dignity is severely tampered, leaving a little human being in cold and isolated inner turmoil.

I say let's support laws like Erin's Law and organizations like Lauren's Kids, Find the Way, LLC, and NAASCA. Being part of the many groups that speak up against child sexual abuse is encouraged. Unfortunately, we cannot afford to be ashamed to be a part of these associations, which were originally started to say *yes*, it is time that sexual abuse against children stops. Child sexual abuse is just sad and uncontrollably painful for any child to bear.

Any child, whether white, blue, purple, or green, who is a victim of abuse suffers, and their suffering is too detrimental to *not* give them the necessary tools to protect themselves in the first place. There are only three things I know can work to prevent child sexual abuse: talk the real talk; really listen to and respect your child; and, oh yes, show unconditional love.

What does *unconditional love* or *selfless love* really mean? The website A Conscious Rethink gives this definition: "Unconditional love, on the other hand, exists in the absence of any benefit for the lover. It transcends all behavior and is in no way reliant upon any form of reciprocation. It is completely and utterly selfless. It cannot be given in as much as it flows without effort from one's heart rather than coming consciously from one's mind. There is nothing that can stand in the way of unconditional love."[69]

Barry Philipp puts it this way: "Raising a child with unconditional love means that no fear is created in parent-child interactions. To love unconditionally simply means that *parents accept their children completely and without restrictions or stipulations.* There is no spoken (or unspoken) message causing the child to think he must be something other than what he is to be loved. The need for unconditional love begins at conception."[70] For some of us, this unconditional love was never taught

---

[69] . "The True Meaning of Unconditional Love (+ How To Recognize It)," A Conscious Rethink, https://www.aconsciousrethink.com/3871/true-meaning-unconditional-love/.

[70] . Barry Philipp, "Unconditional Love," The Natural Child Project, http://www.naturalchild.org/guest/barry_philipp.html.

or shown, making it so difficult to practice. However, as with anything else, practice makes perfect.

When we speak of unconditional love, we tend to think of adult relationships. We think of this in terms of marriage and so forth, yet when in the process of becoming parents, it is mostly not the case. The thinking process may look more like, *I am the parent, and this will be or is my child; thus, he will follow the rules (my rules). In my home, things will run in this matter.* Yet we do not take the time to analyze what the rules are and where they came from. We fail to ask questions like:

- What is my history?
- What was my upbringing like?
- What did it teach me?
- What works and what doesn't work anymore?
- What is love?
- Did I learn about love, and did I feel worthy?
- What are the rules, and why are they important?
- In what areas do I feel incomplete or somehow shortchanged?
- What parenting style am I more inclined to use and why?
- Is this important for my child?
- Is it necessary, and how do I change the areas I didn't like?
- Was I brought up in an environment in which I felt the true meaning of unconditional love?

These questions can definitely set the stage for change and create a better environment for your child and yourself.

What Is Real Talk?

Talk to your children without using baby talk. Tell them as many times as you can that they should be aware that child sexual abuse takes place and that in your book as a parent or caregiver, there is zero tolerance for anyone attempting to abuse or hurt them in any kind of way. The number-one rule in your house should be self-love/unconditional love. *Let your children know you have their back!* Reiterate that you are on their team and will support them in the decisions they make when faced with someone trying to hurt them in any way. They should be able to talk to you and not fear what your reaction will be.

Clearly let them know that there are rules in your house and that your number-one concern is their safety and overall well-being. Talking to children about the reality of sexual abuse prevalence and giving them the green light to not be afraid to report adults trying to hurt them will not traumatize them; being sexually abused will. This epidemic has destroyed many lives and left too many scars, with many children stripped of a healthy childhood, adolescence, or adult life. I, as a parent, advocate, friend, aunt, colleague, and therapist have *zero tolerance*. And you?

Inquire about different programs and why and how they came to be. For example, Erin's Law was named after childhood sexual assault survivor: author, speaker, and activist Erin Merryn, who is founder and president of Erin's Law, which is registered with the State of Illinois and the IRS as a 501 (K) (4) nonprofit social welfare organization. Erin's organization requires that all public schools in each state that passes it implement a prevention-oriented child sexual abuse program that:

- teaches students in pre-K through fifth grade age-appropriate techniques to recognize child sexual abuse and tell a trusted adult
- educates school personnel about child sexual abuse
- informs parents and guardians of the warning signs of child sexual abuse, plus needed assistance, referral, or resource information to support sexually abused children and their families.

The following state governments have already passed Erin's Law:

- Illinois
- Indiana
- Maine
- Missouri

- Michigan
- Arkansas
- Mississippi
- Nevada

TEACH CHILDREN THAT THEY HAVE RIGHTS

First Focus Campaign for Children: Children Bills of Rights, October 2015, outlines children's rights under three major categories: the right to well-being, the right to social and emotional well-being, and the right to educational and life skills. Although all rights for children are to be exercised, the following should be provided as an introductory letter of presentation to any adult undertaking the task of caring for a child, be it a parent, caretaker, and/or legal guardian.[71]

> **Right to Well-Being**: Emphasize the right to be free from all forms of physical, psychological, sexual abuse, or neglect; right to a safe and healthy environment.

> **Right to Social and Emotional Well-Being**: Emphasize the right to develop a healthy attachment to a parent, legal guardian, or caregiver.

> **Right to Educational and Life Skills**: Emphasize the right to be heard in age-appropriate ways on issues regarding their education; their right to access to training in life skills.

> **Overall**: Emphasize their right to privacy and right to be treated with dignity and respect at all times.

---

[71] . First Focus Campus Campaign for Children, "Children's Bill of Rights," https://campaignforchildren.org/wp-content/uploads/sites/2/2015/10/Childrens-Bill-of-Rights.pdf.

Every individual deserves a somewhat "normal" childhood, and I guess we need to start demanding it by empowering our children to protect themselves. This doesn't just empower our children, it empowers *us* to be the best we can be. This is one of the many ways to thrive.

We, as parents, teachers, or advocates, need to make our children aware that we mean business when we say there's is zero tolerance for child sexual abuse. There is absolutely no room for this in our homes, schools, libraries, or neighborhoods. Children need to be aware that we will back them up no matter what. If children know what steps to take to protect themselves, are educated about sexual abuse, and feel safe with their caretakers/parents, they will speak up if anyone tries to abuse them, *even within their own household.*

Thus, success at preventing sexual abuse starts at home. By teaching via our consistent actions and words that we respect our children's rights and treat them with the utmost respect, we are communicating to them that they are to expect no less from any other individual they encounter. By respecting their rights, we are enabling them to expect to be respected, and they will more than likely be empowered to react and defend themselves in front of anyone who can be a potential perpetrator. This is something that more than likely was denied to us and to many, leaving us at a disadvantage when we became parents ourselves. Thus, it is important to know our children's rights and make sure we practice them consistently as parents, caretakers, teachers, coaches, etc.

Children are to be respected … period! There should be no question of this. In my opinion, not even spanking for discipline should exist, as violence teaches violence, fear teaches fear, and yes, *love teaches love.* We humans have the privilege to communicate verbally, gesturally, through sign language (nonverbal), through music, and in written form, yet violence continues to be the preferred mode of communication for the majority. By seeking your own truth, you will change the way you communicate, and the communication style of those around you.

LOLA LOLA'S CLOSING

Silence in my life was equivalent to the years spent in fear of what others would say or think, of my own shame, my overindulgence with self-pity, and most of all my lack of complete understanding and acceptance of the concepts presented to you in this guide. I considered this a problem I went through, and because I had not solved or completely accepted it, I just could not talk about it. I did the same with all my so-called problems, which I consider now "just experiences."

We have a choice to learn from them to continue with movement—continue to go with the flow that comes with learning from our experiences. In my own journey, I would just have moments of breakdown, but never much talking about anything. Therefore, and in honor of myself first, of my family and friends, and of the many who have had to experience such horrendous abuse, I am writing this guide to communicate that change for the better is possible, as it continues to be possible for me. Following the concept that if you make it in New York you can make it anywhere, I say, if I was able to make it out the most terrifying and devastating of experiences, you can make it too and be truly happy while you are at it.

As citizens, we have the constitutional right to pursue happiness. The day when the doctor sharply pulled out the gauze from my insides, the pain of shame was so profound, I decided that life could take almost anything, but not my love for life or my willingness to pursue happiness. I have made sure that no one can be the owner of that, and through the techniques that I am writing about for you to use, no one except *Lola Lola* is the owner of her happiness and her willingness to love and live to the best of her ability. Who is the owner of your happiness?

Some individuals go out and get plastic surgery or a body augmentation of some kind, thinking this will help them feel better about themselves, and perhaps with a subconscious desire to be noticed more. It can help and can also be life-changing for some time. However, eventually, they may find out that this will bring only temporary changes in their life, such as maybe getting more attention from others.

Yet they may fail to recognize that the attention they need more is from themselves; the long-term life-altering changes come from within. They come from the confrontation you decide to have with yourself that pertains to asking who you really are and investigating your own irrational thoughts, perceptions, and/or feelings that slowly come about because of the violation you endured or from your life experiences.

That honest inner reflection will help you see your true beauty—the beauty that requires no kind of surgical intervention. And with that, I leave you for the next time. I leave you with a new desire to find your true beauty as I have and continue to find each and every day on this planet.

As Paul Loeb wrote in his book *Soul of a Citizen: Living with Conviction in Challenging Times*, "Sociologist Parker Palmer describes the resulting unleashing of truth, vision, and strength in the lives of people like Rosa Parks, Vaclav Havel, Nelson Mandela, and Dorothy Day, who've acted on their deepest beliefs. 'These people,' he wrote, 'have understood that no punishment could be worse than the one we inflict on ourselves by living a divided life.' And nothing could be more powerful than the decision to heal that rift, 'to stop acting differently on the outside from what they knew to be true inside.'"[72] Thus, I call on you to be true to who you truly are and learn to live a whole and not a divided life.

I thought of many things to say in this closing. But all I can say is that I believe in you, and I know and am certain that this self-help guide can be a turning point in your life. Nonetheless, you will need to muster up much courage, love, and patience to remain consistent in your journey toward transitioning into the thriving individual you envision yourself to be. And rest assured that it will impact a great many individuals. Your change may perhaps save a life. I believe saving just one life is surely worth your time, and working on *you* as the domino effect is a factual phenomenon.

And know that you are *not* alone. There is always someone. There is always a reason to keep on going. Remember that when there is a will, there is a way!

---

[72] . Paul Rogat Loeb, *Soul of a Citizen: Living with Conviction in a Cynical Time* (New York: St. Martin's Griffin, 1999), 24.

ABOUT THE AUTHOR

Yanette Novoa started her education at Miami Dade Community College, graduating with her associate in arts degree in 1996. She is a graduate from the Florida International University (FIU) with a bachelor's in psychology and master's in clinical social work.

She obtained her licensure on April 5, 2013 and she is a current student in the Ph.D. Human Services program at Carlos Albizu University.

She has specialized in Applied Behavior Analysis (ABA) and mental health field and provided individual, family, and group therapy. Yanette Novoa has ample experience working with individuals with developmental/intellectual disabilities and victims of sexual abuse.

Her life experience and expertise in the field have paved the way in the making of this self-help guide. It is intended to instill hope in our communities and—why not?—our nation, in which child sexual abuse continues to be rampant.

Throughout her years experiencing life and providing therapy to adults and children in the same situation, she discovered the importance of coming to terms with yourself and of the impediments that come from pretending to be who you are not.

Not being yourself and feeling unable to be vulnerable enough to talk about your own experiences will hinder you from experiencing the benefits of having a true and substantial relationship with yourself and others. Not to mention that you will prevent others from knowing the essence of the wonderful human being that you are. Likewise, and of utmost importance, it will keep others from learning from your experience, which can perhaps be the turning point where a life is saved. It is her experience that owning up to who you are will take you on a wonderful journey of self-discovery from which you will never want to escape, bringing an infinite amount of peace to your life, reminding you that, *life is beautiful!*

GLOSSARY

Courage   The capacity for action despite a clear understanding of your limitations and past failings.

Denial   The defense mechanism that protects the personality from anxiety or guilt by disavowing or ignoring unacceptable thoughts, emotions, or wishes.

Displacement   A defense mechanism used to reduce anxiety that accompanies certain thoughts, feelings, or wishes by transferring them to another thought, feeling, or wish that is more acceptable or tolerable.

Guilt   Responsibility for a crime or for doing something bad or wrong; a bad feeling caused by knowing or thinking that you did something wrong.

Mantra   A sound, a word, or a phrase that is repeated by someone who is praying or meditating: a word or phrase that is repeated.

Optimism   A feeling or belief that good things will happen in the future; a feeling or belief that what you hope for will happen.

Patience   The capacity, quality, or fact of being patient.

Rationalization   Presenting in logical terms, or interpreting the reasons for, some action or event; a defense mechanism in which a person explains or justifies an action or thought to make it acceptable when it is unacceptable at a deeper psychological level.

Repression	A defense mechanism derived from psychodynamic theory, in which the individual unconsciously pushes out of the consciousness certain memories, ideas, or desires that are unacceptable or cause an important level of anxiety.
Resiliency	The human capacity (individual, group, and/or community) to deal with crises, stressors, and normal experiences in an emotionally and physically healthy way; an effective coping style. For example, a successfully resilient child might deal with parental neglect and a hostile environment by cultivating healthy relationships with other relatives or friends, whereas one who is not might withdraw and become isolated and lonely.
Self-concept	The idea you have about the kind of person you are.
Self-esteem	A feeling of having respect for yourself and your abilities.
Self-respect	Pride in oneself; respect for or favorable opinion of oneself.
Silence	The condition or quality of being or keeping still and silent; the absence of sound; stillness.
Suppression	In psychosocial theory, the conscious psychic mechanism of putting unpleasant thoughts out of one's mind. The suppression is like repression, except that the latter is a defense mechanism operating unconsciously to remove threatening ideas from one's awareness.

Tolerance   Willingness to accept feelings, habits, or beliefs that are different from your own; willingness to tolerate something, the existence of opinions or behavior with which one does not necessarily agree. Two words to think about during and after your journey that you should always be familiar with and use: resiliency and tolerance. *Can I deal with this crisis? Do I have self-resilience and tolerance?* Do you tolerate yourself?

Victim   A person who has been attacked, injured, robbed, or killed by someone else.

RESOURCES

Prevention, Self-Improvement, and/or Recovery Programs

American Association of Suicidology, www.suicidology.org

Butterfly Dreams Abuse Recovery, https://butterflydreamsabuserecovery.blogspot.com/

Childhelp, https://www.childhelp.org/ 1-800-4.A. child (1-800-422-4453

Child Molestation Research and Prevention Institute, https://www.childmolestationprevention.org/

Child Welfare Information Gateway https://www.childwelfare.gov/topics/preventing/prevention-programs/sexualabuse/

Crimes against Children Research Center https://www.unh.edu/ccrc/

Darkness to Light https://www.d2l.org/

Dr. James Hollis, https://jameshollis.net/hollisBooks.html (resources pertinent to depression, anxiety, life changes)

Erin's Law, educational https://www.dibbleinstitute.org/free-resources/toolkits/erins-law-child-sexual-abuse-prevention-toolkit/

Florida Council Against Sexual Violence, https://www.fcasv.org/, hotline 1-888-956-rape (7273)

Florida Department of Health, https://www.floridahealth.gov/

Lauren's Kids Mission, https://laurenskids.org/ To prevent childhood sexual abuse through education and awareness, and to help survivors heal with guidance and support. Call for help 24/71-877-lkids-01 (it is ok to tell).

Louise Hay, https://www.louisehay.com/

Miami Dade Portal, miamidade.gov/ … /victim-adult/www.teachmore lovemore.org.healthsafe

National Abuse Hotline, 1-800-799-7233

National Association of Adult Survivors of Child Abuse, http://www.naasca.org/

National Center for Missing and Exploited Children, https://www.missingkids.org/education/training/codeadam

National Child Abuse Hotline, 1-800-4-A-Child

National Children's Alliance, https://www.nationalchildrensalliance.org/

National Sexual Assault Hotline, 1-800-656-hope

National Suicide Prevention Lifeline, 1-800-273-talk (8255); https://988lifeline.org/

Prevent Child Abuse America, https://preventchildabuse.org/what-we-do/

RAIN, Rape, Abuse, Incest, National Network, RAINN.org, 800-656-HOPE (4673) https://www.rainn.org/resources

Rape Treatment Center (Jackson Memorial Hospital), 305-585-7273

SECASA, https://www.secasa.org.au/ (https://www.secasa.org.au/wp-content/uploads/2020/10/the-aftermath-of-sexual-assault-am-i-supposed-to-feel-this-way.pdf)

Stop It Now, https://www.stopitnow.org/

The Rape Recovery Handbook*: Step-by-Step Help for Survivors of Sexual Assault* by Aphrodite T. Matsakis, Ph.D.

US Department of Health and Human Services, https://www.hhs.gov/

Note: Anybody who expresses suicidal thoughts or intentions should be taken seriously. Do not hesitate to call your local suicide hotline: 1-800-suicide (1-800-784-2433) or 1-800-273-talk (1-800-273-8255) or the deaf hotline at 1-800-799-4TTY (1-800-799-4889).

Printed in the United States
by Baker & Taylor Publisher Services